WHEN THE CHRIST CAME

THE HIGHLANDS OF GALILEE

The Bible for School and Home

by J. Paterson Smyth

The Book of Genesis

Moses and the Exodus

Joshua and the Judges

The Prophets and Kings

*When the Christ Came:
The Highlands of Galilee*

*When the Christ Came:
The Road to Jerusalem*

St. Matthew

St. Mark

WHEN THE CHRIST CAME

THE HIGHLANDS OF GALILEE

by

J. Paterson Smyth

YESTERDAY'S CLASSICS

ITHACA, NEW YORK

This edition, first published in 2017 by Yesterday's Classics, an imprint of Yesterday's Classics, LLC, is an unabridged republication of the text originally published by Sampson Low, Marston & Co., Ltd. For the complete listing of the books that are published by Yesterday's Classics, please visit www.yesterdaysclassics. com. Yesterday's Classics is the publishing arm of the Baldwin Online Children's Literature Project which presents the complete text of hundreds of classic books for children at www.mainlesson.com.

ISBN: 978-1-63334-029-9

Yesterday's Classics, LLC
PO Box 339
Ithaca, NY 14851

CONTENTS

CONTENTS

GENERAL INTRODUCTION

I

This series of books is intended for two classes of teachers:

1. *For Teachers in Week Day and Sunday Schools.* For these each book is divided into complete lessons. The lesson will demand preparation. Where feasible there should be diligent use of commentaries and of any books indicated in the notes. *As a general rule* I think the teacher should not bring the book at all to his class if he is capable of doing without it. He should make copious notes of the subject. The lesson should be thoroughly studied and digested beforehand, with all the additional aids at his disposal, and it should come forth at the class warm and fresh from his own heart and brain. But I would lay down no rigid rule about the use of the Lesson Book. To some it may be a burden to keep the details of a long lesson in the memory; and, provided the subject has been very carefully studied, the Lesson Book, with its salient points carefully marked in coloured pencil, may be a considerable help. Let each do what seems best in his particular case, only taking care to satisfy his conscience that it is not done through

1

laziness, and that he can really do best for his class by the plan which he adopts.

2. *For Parents* who would use it in teaching their children at home. They need only small portions, brief little lessons of about ten minutes each night. For these each chapter is divided into short sections. I should advise that on the first night only the Scripture indicated should be read, with some passing remarks and questions to give a grip of the story. That is enough. Then night after night go on with the teaching, taking as much or as little as one sees fit.

I have not written out the teaching in full as a series of readings which could be read over to the child without effort or thought. With this book in hand a very little preparation and adaptation will enable one to make the lesson more interesting and more personal and to hold the child's attention by questioning. Try to get his interest. Try to make him talk. Make the lesson conversational. Don't preach.

II

HINTS FOR TEACHING

An ancient Roman orator once laid down for his pupils the three-fold aim of a teacher:

1. *Placere* (to interest).

2. *Docere* (to teach).

3. *Movere* (to move).

1. To interest the audience (in order to teach them).

2. To teach them (in order to move them).

3. To move them to action.

On these three words of his I hang a few suggestions on the teaching of this set of Lessons.

1. Placere (to interest)

I want especially to insist on attention to this rule. Some teachers seem to think that to interest the pupils is a minor matter. It is not a minor matter and the pupils will very soon let you know it. Believe me, it is no waste of time to spend hours during the week in planning to excite their interest to the utmost. Most of the complaints of inattention would cease at once if the teacher would give more study to rousing their interest. After all, there is little use in knowing the facts of your subject, and being anxious about the souls of the pupils, if all the time that you are teaching, these pupils are yawning and taking no interest in what you say. I know some have more aptitude for teaching than others. Yet, after considerable experience of teachers whose lesson was a weariness to the flesh, and of teachers who never lost attention for a moment, I am convinced, on the whole, that the power to interest largely depends on the previous preparation.

Therefore do not content yourself with merely studying the teaching of this series. Read widely and freely. Read not only commentaries, but books that will give local interest and colour—books that will throw valuable sidelights on your sketch.

But more than reading is necessary. You know the meaning of the expression, *"Put yourself in his place."* Practise that in every Bible story, using your imagination, living in the scene, experiencing, as far as you can, every feeling of the actors. To some this is no effort at all. They feel their cheeks flushing and their eyes growing moist as they project themselves involuntarily into the scene before them. But though it be easier to some than to others, it is in some degree possible to all, and the interest of the lesson largely depends on it. I have done my best in these books to help the teacher in this respect. But no man can help another much. Success will depend entirely on the effort to "put yourself in his place."

In reading the Bible chapter corresponding to each lesson, I suggest that the teacher should read part of the chapter, rather than let the pupils tire themselves by "reading round." My experience is that this "reading round" is a fruitful source of listlessness. When his verse is read, the pupil can let his mind wander till his turn comes again, and so he loses all interest. I have tried, with success, varying the monotony. I would let them read the first round of verses in order; then I would make them read out of the regular order, as I called their names; and sometimes, if the lesson were long, I would again and again interrupt by reading a group of verses myself, making remarks as I went on. To lose their interest is fatal.

I have indicated also in the lessons that you should not unnecessarily give information yourself. Try to question it *into* them. If you tell them facts which they have just read, they grow weary. If you ask a question, and then answer it yourself when they miss it, you cannot keep their attention. Send your questions around in every sort of order, or want of order. Try to puzzle them—try to surprise them. Vary the form of the question, if not answered, and always feel it to be a defeat if you ultimately fail in getting the answer you want.

2. *Docere (to teach)*

You interest the pupil in order that you may *teach*. Therefore teach definitely the Lesson that is set you. Do not be content with interesting him. Do not be content either with drawing spiritual teaching. Teach the facts before you. Be sure that God has inspired the narration of them for some good purpose.

When you are dealing with Old Testament characters, do not try to shirk or to condone evil in them. They were not faultless saints. They were men like ourselves, whom God was helping and bearing with, as He helps and bears with us, and the interest of the story largely depends on the pupil realizing this.

In the Old Testament books of this series you will find very full chapters written on the Creation, the Fall, the Flood, the election of Jacob, the Sun standing still, the slaughter of Canaanites, and other such subjects. In connection with these I want to say something that especially concerns teachers. Your pupils, now or later, can hardly avoid coming in contact with the flippant scepticism so common nowadays, which makes jests at the story of the sun standing still, and talks of the folly of believing that all humanity was condemned because Eve ate an apple thousands of years ago. This flippant tone is "in the air." They will meet with it in their companions, in the novels of the day, in popular magazine articles on their tables at home. You have, many of you, met with it yourselves; you know how disturbing it is; and you probably know, too, that much of its influence on people arises from the narrow and unwise teaching of the Bible in their youth. Now you have no right to ignore this in your teaching of the Bible. You need not talk of Bible difficulties and their answers. You need not refer to them at all. But teach the truth that will take the sting out of these difficulties when presented in after-life.

To do this requires trouble and thought. We have learned much in the last fifty years that has thrown new light for us on the meaning of some parts of the Bible; which has, at any rate, made doubtful some of our old interpretations of it. We must not ignore this. There are certain traditional theories which some of us still insist on teaching as God's infallible truth, whereas they are really only human opinions about it, which may possibly be mistaken. As long as they are taught as human opinions, even if we are wrong, the mistake will do no harm. But if things are taught as God's infallible truth, to be believed on peril of doubting God's Word, it may do grave mischief, if in after-life the pupil find

6

them seriously disputed, or perhaps false. A shallow, unthinking man, finding part of his teaching false, which has been associated in his mind with the most solemn sanctions of religion, is in danger of letting the whole go. Thus many of our young people drift into hazy doubt about the Bible. Then we get troubled about their beliefs, and give them books of Christian evidences to win them back by explaining that what was taught them in childhood was not *quite* correct, and needs now to be modified by a broader and slightly different view. But we go on as before with the younger generation, and expose them in their turn to the same difficulties.

Does it not strike you that, instead of this continual planning to win men back from unbelief, it might be worth while to try the other method of not exposing them to unbelief? Give them the more careful and intelligent teaching at first, and so prepare them to meet the difficulties by-and-by.

I have no wish to advocate any so-called "advanced" teaching. Much of such teaching I gravely object to. But there are truths of which there is no question amongst thoughtful people, which somehow are very seldom taught to the young, though ignorance about them in after-life leads to grave doubt and misunderstanding. Take, for example, the gradual, progressive nature of God's teaching in Scripture, which makes the Old Testament teaching as a whole lower than that of the New. This is certainly no doubtful question, and the knowledge of it is necessary for an intelligent study of

Scripture. I have dealt with it where necessary in some of the books of this series.

I think, too, our teaching on what may seem to us doubtful questions should be more fearless and candid. If there are two different views each held by able and devout men, do not teach your own as the infallibly true one, and ignore or condemn the other. For example, do not insist that the order of creation must be accurately given in the first chapter of Genesis. You may think so; but many great scholars, with as deep a reverence for the Bible as you have, think that inspired writers were circumscribed by the science of their time. Do not be too positive that the story of the Fall *must be* an exactly literal narrative of facts. If you believe that it is I suppose you must tell your pupil so. But do not be afraid to tell him also that there are good and holy and scholarly men who think of it as a great old-world allegory, like the parable of the Prodigal Son, to teach in easy popular form profound lessons about sin. Endeavor in your Bible teaching "to be thoroughly truthful: to assert nothing as certain which is not certain, nothing as probable which is not probable, and nothing as more probable than it is." Let the pupil see that there are some things that we cannot be quite sure about, and let him gather insensibly from your teaching the conviction that truth, above all things, is to be loved and sought, and that religion has never anything to fear from discovering the truth. If we could but get this healthy, manly, common-sense attitude adopted now in teaching the Bible to young people, we should, with

God's blessing, have in the new generation a stronger and more intelligent faith.

3. *Movere (to move)*

All your teaching is useless unless it have this object: to move the heart, to rouse the affections toward the love of God, and the will toward the effort after the blessed life. You interest in order to teach. You teach in order to move. *That* is the supreme object. Here the teacher must be left largely to his own resources. One suggestion I offer: don't preach. At any rate, don't preach much lest you lose grip of your pupils. You have their attention all right while their minds are occupied by a carefully prepared lesson; but wait till you close your Bible, and, assuming a long face, begin, "And now, boys," etc. and straightway they know what is coming, and you have lost them in a moment.

Do not change your tone at the application of your lesson. Try to keep the teaching still conversational. Try still in this more spiritual part of your teaching to question into them what you want them to learn. Appeal to the judgment and to the conscience. I can scarce give a better example than that of our Lord in teaching the parable of the Good Samaritan. He first interested His pupil by putting His lesson in an attractive form, and then He did not append to it a long, tedious moral. He simply asked the man before Him, "Which of these three *thinkest thou?*"—i.e., "What do you think about it?" The interest was still kept up. The man, pleased at the appeal to his judgment, replied promptly, "He that showed mercy on him;" and on the instant came the quick rejoinder, "Go, and do thou likewise." Thus the lesson ends. Try to work on that model.

Now, while forbidding preaching to your pupils, may I be permitted a little preaching myself? This series of lessons is intended for Sunday schools as well as week-day schools. It is of Sunday-school teachers I am thinking in what I am now about to say. I cannot escape the solemn feeling of the responsibility of every teacher for the children in his care. Some of these children have little or no religious influence exerted on them for the whole week except in this one hour with you. Do not make light of this work. Do not get to think, with good-natured optimism, that all the nice, pleasant children in your class are pretty sure to be Christ's soldiers and servants by-and-by. Alas! for the crowds of these nice, pleasant children, who, in later life, wander away from Christ into the ranks of evil. Do not take this danger lightly. Be anxious; be prayerful; be terribly in earnest, that the one hour in the week given you to use be wisely and faithfully used.

But, on the other hand, be very hopeful too, because of the love of God. He will not judge you hardly. Remember that He will bless very feeble work, if it be your best. Remember that He cares infinitely more for the children's welfare than you do, and, therefore, by His grace, much of the teaching about which you are despondent may bring forth good fruit in the days to come. Do you know the lines about "The Noisy Seven"?—

"I wonder if he remembers—
    Our sainted teacher in heaven—
The class in the old grey schoolhouse,
    Known as the 'Noisy Seven'?

"I wonder if he remembers
    How restless we used to be.
Or thinks we forget the lesson
    Of Christ and Gethsemane?

"I wish I could tell the story
    As he used to tell it then;
I'm sure that, with Heaven's blessing,
    It would reach the hearts of men.

"I often wish I could tell him,
    Though we caused him so much pain
By our thoughtless, boyish frolic,
    His lessons were not in vain.

"I'd like to tell him how Willie,
    The merriest of us all,
From the field of Balaclava
    Went home at the Master's call.

"I'd like to tell him how Ronald,
    So brimming with mirth and fun,
Now tells the heathen of India
    The tale of the Crucified One.

"I'd like to tell him how Robert,
    And Jamie, and George, and 'Ray,'
Are honoured in the Church of God—
    The foremost men of their day.

"I'd like, yes, I'd like to tell him
    What his lesson did for me;
And how I am trying to follow
    The Christ of Gethsemane.

"Perhaps he knows it already,
    For Willie has told him, maybe,
That we are all coming, coming
    Through Christ of Gethsemane.

"How many besides I know not
    Will gather at last in heaven,
The fruit of that faithful sowing,
    But the sheaves are already seven."

OUR LORD'S PREPARATION AND EARLY MINISTRY

HOW THE CHRIST-CHILD CAME

St. Luke II. 1-17.

The teacher should dwell on the age-long preparation for the coming of Christ and emphasise and explain the few prophecies here quoted. Try to leave the impression of God's great design waiting through ages for its fulfilment.

This is the Fifth Course of our Lessons, The Bible for School and Home.

We have come now to the most solemn and wonderful and important part of all our teaching of the Bible. This is the climax. Everything before was but leading up to this, the most tremendous thing in all history. The Son of God actually coming down from that great kindly world beyond the stars which had been watching sorrowfully the sins and struggles of men—actually coming down himself to live with us, to die for us, to reveal to us the tenderness of the love of God. "I am troubled about them," He said. "I cannot bear to let them perish. They will not listen to the prophets and

15

teachers. I must go down myself. When once they know how much God cares, that must touch their hearts."

This is the most interesting and wonderful story in the world. But to keep up its interest and its wonder, two things are necessary. (1) We must exert our imaginations to picture vividly the scenes, and try to live in them, as it were, so as to escape the deadness which comes from knowing the story already. But also (2) we must take care in our vivid picturing not to become too familiar, not to think of "the Boy Jesus" as lightly as we should think of a boy in the next street. Must remind ourselves of His being God, and of solemn meaning of the Miraculous Birth—God becoming manifest in the flesh.

§ 1. Prophecies of the Coming

If writing your life, what first? Birth. Yes, that is the beginning of you. Is that so of our Lord? (John xvii. 5). Millions of ages before the world was—so far back that brain reels at the thought—still He was there. He was God. Was He at Creation? (John i. 1-3). And at the sad fall which we thought of? Was He sorry? Then began His promises that He would come and help up the poor world again.

These hints and promises coming down through the ages created in the Jews a strong expectation that some day a great Deliverer should come. They did not understand clearly. They were confused. And since they were not very good people, many of them rather expected that it should be some human king or leader who should fight great battles for them and make them victorious over all their enemies. This made trouble when Jesus came to earth and disappointed them by not leading them out to earthly triumph. But the best and holiest had higher thoughts though they, too, did not quite understand.

The Old Testament has many hints of His coming through types and ceremonies and prophecies, etc. We have only time to glance at a few.

First comes that prophecy to the early world (Genesis iii. 15). The seed of the woman shall bruise the serpent's head and the serpent shall bruise his heel. What would that mean? Who was the serpent? And how did men kill a serpent? By bruising his head, *i.e.,* the Coming One should crush the devil and destroy his power but He should suffer in doing it. The serpent shall bruise His heel.

Now look a long way forward. God chose out one nation to teach religion to the world. And God chose a great good man, Abraham, to be the religious head of the young nation. What did He promise? "In thee and in thy seed shall all the nations of the earth be blessed" (Genesis xii. 3; xxii. 18). Don't you think that would mean that One of his race should be a great blessing to the world?

Now we pass over most of the Old Testament types and prophecies—we have not time for them—and just look at some of the hints given by the great prophet Isaiah (Isaiah ix. 6, 7; xxxii. 1 and especially ch. liii). With such hints and prophecies through the Old Testament you can understand why the Jews expected some Great One to come—the Messiah they called Him. (Teacher should read and put special emphasis on Isaiah liii. If there is not time he might merely read the other two.)

So for centuries the world went on and still He did not come. But the world was waiting. And God was preparing all the time, watching the world, getting all things ready. At last "fulness of time come" (Galatians iv. 4), when our story to-day begins. All the separate little nations welded into one great Roman empire, with its one language; with its splendid roads reaching everywhere from Rome; with the people getting worse and more in need of the Christ. Everything ready for founding of His Kingdom. And people seemed to feel that the King must be coming. Everywhere amongst the Jews an excited expectancy. When John the Baptist came "all men mused in their hearts if he were the Christ or not." "Tell us, art thou Elijah who should prepare the way?" "Art thou the Christ?" And John asks of Jesus, "Art thou He that should come?" Evidently there was an attitude of tense expectation (see St. Luke iii. 15).

§ 2. Nazareth

At last "in the fulness of time" God sent forth His Son. The Christ came! To-day we have the story of His coming. A simple, beautiful story. A betrothed couple in a country village of Nazareth. Ever see village carpenter's shop? Where? Describe? Like that, a village workshop in the Nazareth street, and a strong, broad-shouldered carpenter working at his bench with saw and hammer and chisel, making tables and chairs, and ploughs and cattle-yokes for the country-people. Working hard and joyfully to prepare a new home. Why? Engaged to be married soon. To whom? Living in other end of village with her mother, working in the house, making bread, and spinning, and drawing water from the well with other village girls in the evenings. Don't you think she was very beautiful? At any rate, surely beautiful in soul, gentle and modest, loving and religious.

And Joseph the carpenter loved her dearly. I think he was older than she was, and he was very tender to her, and liked to watch her passing, and liked to think of the little home he was making for her. And it must have been pleasant to her to meet him, and to hear him talk of all his brave hopes and plans for their future. I think, too, they cared so much for religion, that they often talked of God's promise of the Messiah. And I can imagine the girl going home after her talks, and kneeling down at her bedside to pray for God's blessing on her lover's life and her own. Little she dreamed how wonderful would be the answer.

Then came a day that she could never forget.

One day—perhaps at prayer—suddenly a wonderful visitor. Who? (Luke i. 26). What did he announce? Think of the awe, and astonishment, and trembling joy? She to be the mother of the Messiah that all the nation hoped for. Fancy her excitement! So the angel departed and she remained awestruck, wondering, thinking, hoping—pondering in her heart. And so the months passed on.

§ 3. The Manger at Bethlehem

I think it must have been she herself through whom
St. Luke learned the story how the Lord Jesus was born.
Try to make a picture of it in your minds. On the valley
road to Bethlehem a straggling procession of travellers
and amongst them a young countrywoman wearily
riding, with her husband beside her leading the ass. "For
there had gone out a decree from Cæsar Augustus that
all the world should be enrolled. And Joseph also went
up from Nazareth unto the city of David which is called
Bethlehem to enrol himself with Mary his betrothed
wife being great with child."

So they draw near to Bethlehem through a land
alive with historic memories. In the pastures beside
them Ruth long ago gleaned in the fields of Boaz. In the
hollow to the right outside the gate brave men had died
to bring David a drink from the Well of Bethlehem. A
little off the road is a memorial sacred to all Jews, where
the light of Jacob's life went out when "Rachel died by me
in the land of Caanan and I buried her by the roadside
on the way to Ephrath (which is Bethlehem)."

But they had greater thoughts in their minds. And
also Mary is getting very tired and there is anxiety about
lodgings. For the travellers for the census have crowded
the town and they hear that there is no room even in
the inn. They were glad to take refuge at last in one
of the natural caves in the hillside where cattle were
bedded. And there, with no kindly woman's hand to aid
her, came the pains of childbirth on that lonely woman
and "she brought forth her son and wrapped Him in

swaddling clothes"—there was no one else to do it—and laid him in the manger for His first infant sleep.

Did ever baby enter this world in lowlier guise? And do we not all love Him the more for it? Somehow it would spoil the picture if He had been born in a palace with princesses to wait on Him and high priests in attendance. That poor little baby whom nobody noticed comes to us in His helplessness with such clinging appeal as if trusting himself utterly to us, as if bidding for our affection, wanting us to be fond of Him. So touchingly, appealingly, did the Christ-child come.

§ 4. The Angels' Christmas Anthem

But that is only half the story of His birthday. The angels are coming in. You remember how we thought of that great kindly world above that sent the Lord Jesus to us. How they must have watched and looked forward to this! For every incoming of God into human life, every spiritual uplift which this world receives is begun in that kindly world before we know anything about it here.

Simply, ordinarily as the coming of the dawn, happened this tremendous thing in the history of the universe, the coming of the Lord of Glory into human life. On the earthly side just a stable, a manger, the cattle in the stalls, a woman wrapping her baby in swaddling clothes. Nothing of wonder in it. Nothing of awe. Until the world from which He came flashes in upon the scene where high over the stable outside in the starlight was the heavenly host stirred to its depths at the coming of the Christ-child.

So we read that lovely story familiar to us all from infancy—how "shepherds were abiding in the field keeping watch over their flocks by night," how the heavenly music swelled and died over the pasture fields of Bethlehem with its glad tidings of great joy which should be to all people—how the Angels as they listened could not restrain their delight, breaking forth into the eternal anthem of their world above, Glory to God in the Highest!

Let us read over again that little story as we close (Luke ii. 8-14) and try to think why the angels were so glad for us, and why we should be glad for ourselves that Jesus came on that first Christmas night long ago.

QUESTIONS FOR LESSON I

Why were the Jews "in expectation" of Our Lord's coming?

Tell me some of the prophecies about Our Lord's coming.

Describe the *earthly* scene on that first Christmas.

Describe the *heavenly* side.

Do you think the angels knew of it before that night?

LESSON II

EARLY DAYS

St. Luke II. 40-52.

Last day we thought of the tremendous thing that had happened. The Lord coming down to us from Heaven as a little baby Boy. Very God with the flesh of Very Man wrapped round His Godhead, to grow up amongst us as a man that we might in some degree understand and know and love Him and learn the kindly heart of God towards us.

§ 1. The Virgin Mother "Pondering in Her Heart"

Now Joseph the carpenter and the Blessed Virgin Mother are back home in Nazareth, bringing with them the Holy Child to be reared up to manhood. How we should love to know the story of His childhood, all the delightful little things that mothers love to tell about their children. But I suppose God thought it best that we should not know. The Bible draws a veil over the incidents of His childhood and we are only told that "the Child grew and waxed strong in spirit and the grace of God was upon Him and daily He increased in wisdom and stature and in favour with God and man."

I do not think His mother understood till long afterwards the Great Mystery in which she was taking part. She knew that her child was the destined Messiah, that God had some great purpose for His life. But she could not have known then the tremendous fact that it was the Lord from Heaven in human form that she was carrying in her arms. She only learned all that later on. Else how could He be brought up as a natural human boy? How could she have dealt with Him at all as her child? The thought of His Divinity would have overwhelmed everything and made it impossible to treat Him as human. The family life would have been impossible, inconceivable. The purpose of His Incarnation would have been frustrated that He should become like unto His brethren and grow gradually in human thought and consciousness that He should be Very Man as well as Very God.

No. She could not have known then. She must have been often puzzled. The Gospels repeatedly present her as observing and marvelling and pondering over the events of the Childhood. They suggest a quiet, reticent woman wrapped in loving reverent thought of her mysterious Child, solemnised by the memories of His miraculous birth; seeing the high destiny before Him but not knowing how it should be accomplished, and therefore often puzzled; noting intently the strange things that were happening, trying to fit them into her ideas; thinking and wondering and holding her peace: "Mary kept all these sayings and pondered them in her heart."

§ 2. *Children in the Market Place*

So we think of Him as a natural human boy in a natural human family in that village home in Nazareth by the carpenter's shop. I have been trying to picture Him to myself in that little world. I have hanging in my study a large photograph of Nazareth and its surroundings where I can see the identical mountains and valleys that He saw and the very fields where He walked and the little mountain town nestling white against the dark hills behind.

And so one can in some degree picture His boy life. It needs an effort to pass from thinking of the Eternal Son "whose goings forth are from of old from everlasting" to thinking of and trying to visualise a little Boy in Nazareth going on messages for His mother and sweeping up the shavings in the carpenter's shop—to see Him among the "children playing in the marketplace" the games of the unchanging child world such as our children play to-day. I love to think of Him playing in the marketplace. It brings Him so close to our own children's lives. I came one day on a delightful discovery about this. Just as you hear the children to-day singing in a village street "London Bridge is broken down" and "Round and round the mulberry bush," so two thousand years ago you might have heard the Nazareth children calling to their fellows:—

> We have piped and ye not *räkedtoon*
> We have mourned and ye not *arkedtoon*.

And Jesus remembered that rhyme of His childhood

25

and quoted it one day in a solemn discourse, "Ye are like the children crying in the marketplace

> *"We have piped unto you and ye have not danced*
> *We have mourned unto you and ye have not wept."*

You cannot make it rhyme in English or in Greek, only in the language of the Nazareth children which at once suggests the rhyme of a children's game. I shall never again hear village children singing in the marketplace without thinking of that rhyme and the Child Jesus at play.

§ 3. *The Child's Education*

One likes to think of His religious teaching—of the sacred hours when Mary put her Child to bed, teaching Him his prayers, telling Him of the Father, with the absorbing thought in her heart of the great destiny before Him. How He would go to the synagogue school of the town taught by the country rabbi. The Jews of that day set great importance on the school where the children learned for hymns the simpler psalms, for history the Old Testament stories of God's dealings with Israel. One wonders what sort of man was the old country rabbi who had the teaching of Jesus. Longfellow in the Golden Legend pictures the scene:—

> Come hither, Judas Iscariot,
> See if thy lesson thou hast got
> From the rabbinical book or not:
>
>   *   *   *   *   *
>
> And now little Jesus, the carpenter's son,
> Let us see how thy task is done.

When He could read, the chief, probably the only books He had, would be those of the sacred Scriptures where He learned the very stories that we have of Abraham and Jacob and Joseph in Egypt and the great prophets who taught Israel of holiness and sometimes gave them glimpses of a great Messiah to come.

And I think all the world around, the beautiful Book of Nature would be always teaching Him about God. One feels that a special consciousness of the Father was always with Him. And so as I look at my Nazareth photograph I think of the Boy wandering over those same hills and fields seeing the Father's flowers and birds and beasts and delighting in them and loving them and feeling that the Father in Heaven also delighted in them and loved them. In all His references to Nature afterwards He makes you feel this. God is behind it all, interested in it all. God loves the little lambs sporting in the fields. God watches the poor sheep going astray. God feeds the birds of the air which sow not, neither do they reap. God sees the little sparrow fallen out of the nest. He decks for His pleasure the wild flowers of the hills so that "Solomon in all his glory was not arrayed like one of these."

What a lovely thing a child's religion might be if he could learn it rightly as Jesus would, with the thought of the kindly Father pervading it all. Surely Jesus was a happy child in that free, simple boyhood in Nazareth before the consciousness of the world's pain and sin began to press upon His heart.

§ 4. *"When He Was Twelve Years Old"*

I think we are justified in letting our thoughts dwell lovingly on the childhood of Our Lord. But remember little has been revealed. There is only one break in the long silence as to His early days. We read that Joseph and Mary went up every year to the Passover, and when He was twelve years old He went up with them to the Feast (Luke ii. 41).

Surely for the Boy a time to be remembered. His first sight of sacred Jerusalem. His solemn thoughts as He entered the stately Temple, the House of His Father, the centre of Israel's worship all the world over, the vast crowds, a million of Jews from every nation under Heaven come together with one intent—to worship the Father in His holy Temple. And then the rabbis. Here was His young soul thirsting for knowledge, starved, perhaps, by the ignorant old rabbi in Nazareth. Here were the great teachers of the nation—the men who knew! We learn of the Boy's intense interest in the teaching and the questions He asked, until at last the rabbis began to notice Him and get interested in Him and finally to "wonder at His understanding and answers."

I wish we knew what He asked them. I wish we knew more about the matter altogether. But the story has probably come through His mother and she only came in at the close looking for her lost Child. We read that she reproached Him for the anxiety He had caused by His absence and then we have the first recorded words of Jesus, "Why, mother, how is it that you are surprised?

Should you not expect to find me here occupied in the things of my Father in the house of my Father?"

"And they understood not the things which He spake unto them. But His mother kept all these sayings in her heart." You see she did not understand. And the Boy had to think out His thoughts alone. The beginning of the loneliness of Jesus.

We do not understand either. It looks as if it were a crisis in His young life. Maybe the slumbering instinct of the Eternal was awakening in the Child, lighting up the dim consciousness in Him already that He was somehow different from those about Him, from the children He played with and the parents who reared Him. If so it gives more emphasis to the next little statement. "He went down with them and came to Nazareth and was subject unto them." Which brings a lesson for us all. We might well feel that such high thoughts and high happenings would make the monotony of village life distasteful. But the Divine Child had learned and hereby teaches us that simple obedience and dull occupations may be still more high and holy in the sight of the Father. For Him at present that daily life was "His Father's business." For He was only twelve and the simple obedience of the home life was doubtless the best preparation for His future. No unnatural stimulation should be His, no precocious growth, no flattery or admiration. He was to grow to manhood unnoticed, unknown. His life was to develop naturally, normally, wholesomely.

§ 5. *The Carpenter*

So the curtain falls again upon His life. For twenty years more He lived unknown, working as a carpenter in Joseph's workshop. We believe that when Joseph died and the lonely widow had sobbed out her grief in the arms of her beloved Son then He had to work on to support His mother. "Is not this the carpenter, the Son of Mary?" We dare not try to follow the great thoughts stirring in Him as He wrought at the bench all day or climbed in the evening the Nazareth hills, contemplating in solitude the mystery of His future or staying as in later days on the mountain top "continuing all night in prayer to God."

Thus we leave Him till His great call came.

QUESTIONS FOR LESSON II

Did Jesus remember in later life the time when He played with the children in the marketplace?

Can you tell anything about His religious education?

What could He learn from Nature around Him?

Tell fully what happened when He was twelve years old.

Why is He called The Carpenter?

LESSON III

THE BAPTISM AND TEMPTATION

Read St. Matthew III. and IV. to v. 12.

§ 1. *Two Boys Growing Up*

Eighteen years have passed since the Boy Jesus returned from that exciting week in Jerusalem with the rabbis and came back to His life discipline in the quiet, obscure village of Nazareth. The Boy has become a Man. Thirty years old. Working at the carpenter's bench to support His widowed mother—reading His great Books—thinking His great thoughts—waiting.

All these years another boy has been growing up—born the same year as He in a clergyman's house on the wild hills of Hebron. You remember how the Virgin Mother, after the angel's visit, hurried off to tell her cousin Elizabeth in Hebron. Elizabeth, too, was about to become a mother and there were strange prophecies about her unborn child, that he should one day become a prophet in Israel, to be a herald of the coming Messiah, to "prepare the way of the Lord."

31

That boy has also grown to manhood, a hermit in the wilderness, an enthusiast with the dreamer's eyes—in fasting and penitence seeking self-mastery, clothing himself in hair-cloth, feeding on beggar's food of locusts and wild honey. And all the time meditating on the utterances of the prophets, especially on that mysterious line of thought running like a golden thread through the web of prophecy—the dream of a Golden Age, a Kingdom of God, a day in the future when some great Coming One should come. At last his time came. "Now in the fifteenth year of Tiberius Cæsar . . . the Word of God came to John, the son of Zacharias, in the wilderness. And he came into all the region round about Jordan preaching the baptism of repentance as is written in the book of Isaiah the prophet, 'The voice of one crying in the wilderness, Make ready the way of the Lord.'"

In a few months the whole country is ringing with the rumour of him. Excited voices are crying in Jerusalem itself, "We have heard him. We have seen him. He is Elijah come back. He is denouncing our sins. He is saying startling things about Him who is to come!"

§ 2. *The Baptism of Jesus*

Our Lord must have felt now that He can stay no longer. His time is come. Patiently for thirty years He has waited. Now the Divine longing must have its way. He must go out to lift up the poor world.

So one day, in His simple dress, He suddenly appears in the crowd listening to John at Jordan. Describe scene before Him. What was John like? The crowd? Listening, do you think? Ah! they had to listen there. Whenever a great soul like that, full of enthusiasm for his message, thinking not of advancement or praise, of fine clothes, giving up everything in his eager excitement to rouse men to righteousness—people can't help listening. No gentle preacher was he. "Away with your hypocrisies and shams and unrealities. For Messiah is coming whose fan is in his hand. He shall winnow the chaff from the wheat, the shams from the realities. And think not to say within yourselves, We have Abraham to our father, for God is able of these stones to raise up children to Abraham. No. I am not Messiah. I am not that prophet. I am but a voice crying in the wilderness, Prepare ye the way of the Lord."

All this time Jesus was in the crowd, quietly awaiting His turn, standing in His simple country dress by the river. Now He comes down. Did He come confessing His sins, like the rest? Why not? What did John say? Do you think John knew Him to be the Christ? (John i. 33). But he knew his cousin as the truest, noblest heart on earth, in whom no man had ever seen meanness, or selfishness, or any sin. So felt unworthy to baptise Him. Now tell me of baptism, and the wonderful event, the crowning of the King from Heaven. The heavens opened and a vision as of a Dove lighted upon Jesus and a voice was heard from heaven, a voice Divine, "This is my beloved Son in whom I am well pleased." Did the crowd see and hear it? We don't know. Did John? (John i. 33). Astonished, struck dumb with reverence and awe, he saw his young carpenter cousin claimed as

God. Like as if, when Peter the Great was working in an English dockyard in disguise, the Court of Russia should suddenly appear and crown him amid his workmen-companions. Then John knew of a certainty that he had found the Christ.

§ 3. *"Led Up into the Wilderness"*

The next chapter brings a startling change. It is just after the Baptism. Straight from the opened heaven and the voice of the Father, Jesus is "led up into the wilderness to be tempted of the devil." Its prominence in the gospels makes it quite clear that this was a solemn and most important crisis in the life of Jesus. We can only guess at its full significance. It would seem that He was meditating on His tremendous life-work, facing its perplexities, seeking the way out and that Satanic agencies of awful power were struggling with Him, trying to tempt, to mislead, to deflect Him from His course. He who became man to found the Kingdom of God must begin by encountering and defeating as man the powers of the Kingdom of Evil.

§ 4. *"To Be Tempted of the Devil"*

Evening come. Crowd departed. John has retired to his cave in awe and wonder. And Jesus departed, too, alone. Where? Away, away out into wild desert country. Could not rest. Great thoughts and yearnings stirring in His soul. His whole life stirred to its foundation by this wondrous scene. The spirit of God pressing powerfully on Him. He must be away, alone in communion with His father. Away, away through the starry night, into the trackless desert, not thinking of danger, nor of the wild beasts, nor of hunger, nor of anything, but the great, wonderful thoughts that are filling His soul.

And while wrapped in His great future, and His communion with God, and His delight in the self-sacrifice for men, a horrible thing happens. Evil spirits crowd in on Him, struggling, tempting, tormenting, trying to lead Him wrong. That must have been an awful forty days. So strained is He with the conflict that He forgets to eat—for how long? People in intense mental excitement often forget to eat.

But when excitement over, there comes terrible reaction; feels weak, and tired, and despondent. Very hard time to resist temptation. This time, therefore, chosen by Satan for his most powerful attacks. Why attack Christ? If he can make Him sin, it will spoil His power. Whether Satan came as a great black angel of evil, or whether visible at all, we don't know. Do you remember story of his first coming to man? (Genesis iii.) Did he ever come to you? Visible? How? Perhaps like that to Jesus. We don't know. Perhaps the Evangelists themselves did not know. Who must have given account of the Temptation? Why? Because no one else knew but He. And whether the tempter visible or not, Christ says he was the devil. Think of this when you feel him tempting you. A great, real, wicked devil. Don't say, "I feel bad desires and thoughts," but say, "I am tempted of the devil," like our Lord, and rise up and fight him bravely in the strength which our Lord will give you.

Remember, too, Jesus had to fight him *as a man*. He had "emptied Himself." There would have been no need to show that as God He could triumph over Satan. But He had come down to our level as our brother, and would take no advantage that we could not have. Like an armoured knight of old, fighting in front of his peasant soldiers, but putting away his armour, and shield, and horse, and fighting just as they, to inspirit them.

§ 5. *The Temptations*

What was the first temptation? Could He do it? Was it a sore temptation? What harm would it have been? We don't quite know. Perhaps because He was our brother, must fight like His brothers, and trust in God. Never use for His own gain the Divine power. Would be like the knight, when in danger, saving himself by putting on his armour, which his poor brethren could not have. No, He would trust in God; and into His mind at once flashed a verse, which perhaps He had learned in the old rabbi's village school. What was it? "Man shall not," etc. Good thing in temptation to know one's Bible.

Then Satan, seeing His trust, very cunningly tries to tempt him that way. Second temptation? Yes. "Trust God to keep you if you throw yourself off temple." Why should not He? Because it is only in the path of duty we may trust God. If anything be our duty, do it, even at risk of life, and trust God. But not if go into needless danger, doing your own will, to win admiration or recognition from others. What text quoted?

36

Third temptation? I don't quite understand how this could be a temptation. What did Jesus care about earthly glory, and money, and power? Perhaps this was a stupid blunder of Satan. He was very cunning and subtle; but low, degraded souls cannot understand high and noble souls. Very cunning, tricky, self-seeking man, who could "buy and sell" the wisest around him, yet would be quite unable to understand an utterly noble, unselfish man, full of enthusiasm for God and self-sacrifice. And so would not know how to tempt such a one. Perhaps it was that. But more probably he thought Jesus so anxious to get the kingdoms to bless them, that He would be willing to "do evil that good might come." Would He? What was the third answer from Scripture?

Then what happened? (*v.* 11). Battle over, victory won. Did it ever happen with you? Try to make it happen, and you will learn that the devil is a bully and a coward. Like a bully at school, squaring up to a small boy to frighten him; but if small boy hits back, the bully runs away. So Satan (James iv. 7). It is a great delight to drive him off, one feels so glad, and proud, and thankful. Especially remember that the devil *leaves us*. He is not omnipresent, any more than omnipotent. Some think he is, and they lose heart in temptation, and say: "I may as well give in now as later, for this strain of temptation will be always pressing on me." It is not so. The time of your sharpest temptation is "his hour and the power of darkness." Remember that. Fight through it. And perhaps it will be days and days before a really fierce temptation comes again. Try it next time and you will see how beautifully all our Lord's fight was for your encouragement and example. The devil will leave you, and in the comfort and peace you will feel as if angels were come to minister unto you.

QUESTIONS FOR LESSON III

Who was John the Baptist?

What was he born for?

Describe the Baptism and the wonderful thing that happened.

Why should Satan want to tempt Jesus?

Tell of the three chief temptations.

What did Jesus answer to each?

Since Jesus was God how could His temptation be any example or encouragement to us?

LESSON IV

THE FIRST DISCIPLES

St. John I. 35-51.

To avoid confusion here, carefully distinguish between John the Baptist and John the young disciple. Also emphasise here that this is the first small beginning of Jesus' Kingdom of God on earth.

§ 1. An Old Disciple's Memories

Here comes a delightful little story of how our Lord first met some of the great Apostles of later days. We should never have heard of it if one of these had not told us in his old age, long after the earlier gospels were written. These earlier gospels only tell of the public call of the Twelve. But one of these Twelve many years afterwards as he read these gospels must have said to himself: Ah! they have left out those wonderful days after the temptation. As he read of Jesus publicly calling the Twelve Apostles to their office he thinks: they have not told of those delightful days when some of us first made His acquaintance. So St. John, who fills up many other gaps in the gospel story, fills this gap too.

39

He had intimate memories that the others had not of those precious three years with Jesus on earth. And among all his memories one especially stands out—the memory of a certain afternoon at four o'clock fifty years ago—the hour when he first met his beloved Lord. That is the red-letter day of his life; he cannot have that left out. So he tells what he remembers.

§ 2. An Evening Alone with Jesus

It was just after the Temptation. Six weeks ago Jesus had been baptised and then immediately He was led up into the wilderness to be tempted of the Devil. So He vanished from sight and the Baptist and the others did not know where He had gone to.

Now the Baptist is standing by the river with some of his intimates when suddenly down the path where he had disappeared six weeks ago Jesus appears walking towards them, a tired man surely with the strain of the forty days showing on Him, with the light of another world in His eyes. Immediately the Baptist recognises Him. "Behold the Lamb of God which taketh away the sins of the world. This is He of whom I told you: 'I beheld the Spirit descending on Him as a Dove and I have seen and bear witness that this is the Son of God.'"

The next day John the Baptist is standing with a group of young disciples, young fishermen who had come up from Capernaum to hear him, and young John, the disciple who tells the story, was one of them. Again Jesus passed on the path below. "Look," cries the Baptist, gripping his young companion, "behold the Lamb of God!" And two young fishermen, young John and another, started down the path shyly, timidly, awkwardly, half hoping, fearing that Jesus might turn and speak to them. And He did. Kindly He asks, "Whom seek ye?" They hardly knew what to say. "Master, where dwellest Thou?" Jesus knew the timid thought and wish in their hearts. "Come with me and see."

It was a wonderful happening and the aged disciple looking back over fifty years remembers the very hour of it. "It was about the tenth hour" (four o'clock). Think what it meant to those two to spend that evening with Jesus talking to him naturally, easily. I wonder what he told them and what they asked Him. Maybe He told of His great plan for His Kingdom on earth. Maybe he asked, Will you join me when I am ready? At any rate, I am quite sure that they came back from that visit, their pulses stirring with wonder and enthusiasm, their hearts swelling with a great reverent affection for their new Friend.

§ 3. How Peter Came into the Group

One of them was John and he says that "one of them was Andrew, Simon Peter's brother. Andrew first findeth his own brother Simon and tells him, We have found the Christ!" That is how the famous St. Peter, that affectionate, blundering, great-hearted Peter, first came into the group of the disciples of Jesus.

Don't you love to think of that aged St. John looking back on this delightful memory? And don't you love to think of the way in which Jesus won these young men to him—just by loving them, making friends with Him, letting them get to know Him? One feels that there must have been a delightful charm, a wonderful human attractiveness in Jesus. You could not help loving Him if you knew Him on earth. I do not think any of us could help loving Him now if we only knew Him as He is and knew the thoughts in His heart towards us.

§ 4. *Nathanael*

Next day Jesus is starting for Galilee. He is to stop at Cana for a wedding. And the three young friends go with Him, for they have to go back home to their fishing on the Lake of Galilee and they also are invited to the wedding. On the road they meet Philip, with whom I think the Lord is already acquainted. And when they get to Cana, Philip goes right off to an intimate friend of his, Nathanael Bartholomew. Probably they had often talked together of the coming Messiah.

"Nathanael! we have found Him of whom Moses and the prophets did write."

"Who is He?"

"Jesus of Nazareth, the son of Joseph."

But Nathanael has his doubts. He is a cautious man. He does not expect the Messiah to come in this casual way. He answers in the contemptuous proverb of the day, "Can any good thing come out of Nazareth?"

Philip will not argue with him. "Come out and meet him yourself." So Nathanael came out. And he met Jesus on the road. And I do not think any man of honest and good heart could ever meet Jesus without being immediately attracted to Him. Jesus, too, was attracted by him. "Behold an Israelite," He says, "in whom is no guile!"

"How do you know me?" asks Nathanael.

"I know all about you. Before Philip called you, when you were sitting under the fig-tree, I saw you." Probably they talked further. At any rate Nathanael was immediately won to Him. "Rabbi, thou art the Son of God. Thou art the King of Israel!"

§ 5. *"Touch the Next Man"*

So Jesus has already won four friends who were devotedly attached to Him. He was beginning that little band of men who should go out with Him to win the world for the Kingdom of God. Name these four for me. Is not that a very little beginning for so great a purpose? But that was Jesus' way of beginning. Do you remember in his parables how He prophesies The Kingdom of God is like a little grain of mustard seed, smallest of all seeds, which shall one day grow to be a great tree with the fowls of the air lodging in the branches thereof? Show me now how this parable has to do with this small beginning. He has not yet called them to do anything publicly—just made friends with them on the way. One day they should stand in the great band of the Twelve Apostles.

So Jesus and his four young friends on that country

road were to be the beginning of great things. They would do anything for Him because they already loved and admired Him and would do so more and more as they knew Him better. That is the way He wants us all to work for Him. Begin by getting to know Him. Read about Him in the gospels. Hear about Him in church. And pray to Him to draw you nearer. "Pour into our hearts such love toward thee that we may love thee above all things."

And when we begin to know and love Him we shall soon help others. Have we any part now in building up this Kingdom of God on earth? How? Begin with ourselves. Learn to love Him ourselves. Then what did Andrew do? First findeth his own brother Simon and brought him to Jesus. That is what Jesus wants of you. You can do it without preaching—perhaps without much talking of religion. Just be loving and attractive yourself. Then get a quiet talk to a careless comrade. Ask him to come to church with you next Sunday. Get him attached to his church. And you two by reading about Jesus and praying for His help will get to love Him more, and you two will get others, and they will get others again. And so the Kingdom will be growing. And the dear Lord, looking down, will be pleased with you all.

Now we leave these four with Jesus in Cana. They are going to wait for the wedding to which they are invited on the third day, the day after to-morrow. Next lesson we shall think about that wedding.

QUESTIONS FOR LESSON IV

Who tells the story about these young disciples? When?

Name these first friends of the Lord.

How did St. Peter come in?

What duty does this suggest to us?

THE WEDDING IN CANA OF GALILEE

St. John II. 1-12.

The two main thoughts to be emphasised are (1) the delightful human attractiveness of Jesus whose presence brought happiness wherever He came, and (2) that we are living in a world of God's miracles and wonders of which most of the Bible miracles are only little specimens.

§ 1. A Wedding in the Family

We are still keeping to St. John's story in which he fills some of the gaps left in the earlier gospels. They do not seem to have known of this wedding. At any rate, they do not tell it.

Now do you see anything to suggest that the bride might be a relative of Jesus? The first thing I notice is that the mother of Jesus was very prominent at this wedding. She seems in charge of the arrangements. Evidently it was a wedding in the family. Either the bride or bridegroom was a near relative of Jesus. Perhaps the bride's mother was dead and Mary took her place. Do not you like to think of that little bride with the myrtle wreath in her hair, glad and proud because Jesus had come to her wedding? Probably she had known Him since childhood, as her home was only four miles away. And now on this day of her woman's joy she wanted her Cousin whom she admired and loved as a big elder brother, and who was already being known as a great Teacher sent from God, she wanted Him to honour her wedding and see her happiness and bless her. Therefore, "Jesus was invited and his disciples to the marriage."

Now should you think that Jesus with all His great thoughts and responsibilities and the destiny of the world resting on His shoulders would spend time coming to a little country wedding? But He came. God is interested in our little lives. Jesus loved to make people happy. And I think He enjoyed coming. There was a wonderful human attractiveness in Jesus. He loved coming and the people loved to have Him come. If we were there I think we should have loved it too. Maybe if we studied the story of His life and got to know Him as these people did we could learn to love Him now, too, as those four young disciples did.

§ 2. Was Jesus of a Sad Countenance?

I think Jesus made happiness at that wedding and made happiness wherever He came. I think it is a great pity that the pictures of Him so often are of a sad countenance. I suppose it comes from Isaiah's prophecy of "a man of sorrows and acquainted with grief." The great painters have persistently repeated that in their pictures and so left a wrong impression. True, "He has borne our griefs and carried our sorrows" and was troubled about the sins of the world and died for them at the last. But to feel for others and die for others does not destroy the joy of a great soul. Self-sacrifice to such an one would be a joy in itself. Ask the lad who on the battlefield faced death to bring in a wounded comrade.

Jesus made happiness wherever He came because He was so happy Himself. He laughed pleasantly at weddings. He loved meeting people. He is always cheering up despondent people. Cheer up! He says, be of good cheer. Of course He was happy. The happiest people in the world to-day are the people who are doing most for others, the people who have joyous ideas of God and perfect trust in God, people who know that they must finally succeed, who know that death only means birth into a fuller life and that evil is a thing which one day must vanish forever. None of us could help being happy if we were like Him. Nay, Jesus was not of a sad countenance. We know His personality was very attractive and sad countenances are not very attractive. He did not like them. "When ye fast," He says, "be not of a sad countenance."

§ 3. Jesus Was God

Now how does this thought bring us a happy gospel of God for ourselves? Because Jesus was God. So you learn the kindly nature of the Godhead. God likes weddings. God likes happiness. Watch Jesus at this wedding—happy, human, natural, sympathising with the joy of young lovers in their marriage—and say to yourself, that is God, that is how God feels.

God, of course, cares most of all for holiness and nobleness of life, but God is not a sort of magnified clergyman interested only in churches and prayers and sacraments and standing apart from us in our lighter moments. He is interested in the birds and the flowers and the lambs skipping in the field and the children singing in the marketplace and the boys playing cricket and football and the mother's thought for her baby and the shy young bride meeting her bridegroom. God gave us music and art. God gave us humour and laughter. I think he loves to see us merrily, innocently laughing. If God could only get us to stop doing wrong we should have just a delightful world.

§ 4. About Miracles

Now Jesus at this marriage performed the very first of His miracles, What? Why did He do it? Explain.

I wonder if He had intended this. I do not think so. He seems to have hesitated at first. He had to make a sudden decision. He had not yet begun His public life. To begin miracles was a serious matter. But He knew that His young friends would be shamed before their neighbours for failing in hospitality. A proud Galilean peasant family would feel it deeply. In a moment His decision was made. A week ago He had refused to turn

49

stones into bread to relieve His own hunger. Now He would turn water into wine to relieve the feelings of His humble friends. That is God. That is what God is like.

This leads us to talk about miracles. Do you think it difficult for Our Lord to turn water into wine? Why could He do it? Because He was God. Did He ever do it before? Don't you think He is always doing it? Out in California or Niagara or in the great vineyards of Central Europe, what happens every year? One day I was travelling through the Rhone valley in Switzerland when I thought of this miracle of Cana. It was pouring rain. The slopes of the valley were clothed with vines. The water was falling heavily on the vineyards. And in two months more I knew the vine-gatherers would come and find that water turned into wine. You see? The Lord is always doing miracles much greater than those in the Bible. We read that He once increased five barley loaves to feed five thousand people. But He is always doing that. Out in the great prairies of Canada and western America the farmer puts down one bushel of wheat upon the earth, as upon an altar of God, and then he can do no more. He goes away and waits for God. And God lays His hand on that altar of earth and whispers His message to that buried seed and He sends the rain and the sun and the winds of Heaven. And, lo! in a few weeks little living green shoots arise and when the farmer comes back at harvest to look upon his field he finds fifty bushels of living wheat where the one bushel was laid down!

You see God is always doing miracles. We are living in the midst of miracles. The starry world above us at midnight. The fruits and the flowers and the great yellow harvest to feed the world. God is always doing wonders, and doing them for us. "Oh, that men would therefore praise the Lord for His goodness and the wonders which He doeth for the children of men!"

So the Lord Jesus only did on a very small scale at Cana one of the miracles that He is always doing. And I think that little bride at Cana was very grateful to Him.

QUESTIONS FOR LESSON V

Why do you think the bride at Cana was a relative of the Lord?

What awkward thing happened at the wedding?

Why, do you think, He did it?

Did He ever do it before?

Tell me of His making wine in Italy and multiplying grain on the prairies.

LESSON VI

THE WRATH OF THE LAMB

St. John II. 12-23.

§ 1. Casting Out the Money-Changers

Soon after the wedding the Lord Jesus went on to Capernaum with three of his young disciples who lived there and were going home. (Find Capernaum on a map. I want you to take special notice of it. For though he did not delay there now, it was afterwards His home for more than a year, "His own city," the centre for His Galilean ministry and the scene of the most familiar stories in the gospels.) Thence He went on to Jerusalem to the Passover Feast as He had probably done every year since that first Passover of His boyhood.

A remarkable thing happened at this Passover. The cleansing of the Temple. Our Lord had great reverence for the Temple. It was the centre of the national worship, the visible symbol of the Father's presence. He was very jealous for its honour. And its honour was being degraded by the covetous dealings of the High Priest and his friends. The beautiful outer court was turned into a noisome cattle market, the din of the money-changers, the bleating of sheep and the lowing of oxen disturbed even the devotions of the people in church. They had to have sheep and oxen for the sacrifices, but this was not the place for them and the priests had no business to be grasping cattle dealers. Many of the people were disgusted and angry, but they were afraid of the priests and dared not speak out. No reformer arose with courage to put an end to this.

Now St. John, the young fisherman, was up that week, and long afterwards, in his old age, he remembers and tells the story. This is the picture in his memory:

The city is densely crowded. Hour after hour the Temple is filled and emptied. New worshippers continually moving toward the entrance. But the cattle are trampling and soiling the court and the bargainers are shouting and disturbing the worship. No one has the courage to complain. Suddenly there is a commotion at the gate and all eyes are turned to see the young prophet from Galilee coming in. Already He is being talked about a good deal in the city. He startles them by His entrance. Not the meek and lowly Jesus of our pictures, nor the friendly Jesus of the Cana wedding. Here is a stern, masterful man striding in in imperious anger through the court like a master coming to chastise misbehaving servants.

Sternly He rebukes the rulers of the Temple. "Take these things hence. Make not my Father's house a house of merchandise!" The priests are astonished and enraged. No one has ever dared to beard them like this. They remonstrate, but He is too angry to listen. "Take these things hence. It is written, My house shall be called a house of prayer, but ye have made it a den of thieves!"

Surely it made a sensation in Jerusalem. Everyone was talking of it. How do you think the people felt? Yes. Startled and half frightened at the daring attack, but surely in their hearts pleased and proud that somebody had dared where they themselves were afraid. And what do you think the priests would feel? Aye. Hatred. The beginning of that long fierce dislike that ultimately brought the Lord to Calvary.

§ 2. Times When Jesus Was Angry

Now here is surely a valuable lesson about anger. Is anger usually a good thing? Is it ever? Do you like or dislike the anger of Our Lord? Why? Because it was righteous, unselfish anger, anger for sake of others, for sake of God and religion. Anger in such a case is surely right. We should think less of a man who was not angry then.

I think there is danger of misunderstanding in the usual pictures of Our Lord with gentle loving face and the usual teaching about His meekness and love. How? Don't you see? They make a false one-sided picture that does not always appeal to us. We feel that love with no capacity for hatred and anger seems a weak, colourless thing. We feel that in a strong man's life there are times for stern anger that makes men afraid. And we are right. For Jesus who alone exhibited perfect manhood was again and again angry. Tell me some times when He

54

was angry? When a set of narrow bigots with their petty little rules tried to keep Him from healing a suffering man on the Sabbath. "He looked round on them with anger" (Mark iii. 5). He is angry at the thought of one seducing one of His little ones to sin. "It were better that a millstone were tied around his neck and that he were drowned" (Matthew xviii. 6). He was awfully angry at the tyranny and hypocrisy of priests that kept men back from God. "Woe unto you Scribes and Pharisees, ye hypocrites, ye blind guides, ye whited sepulchres! Ye serpents, ye generation of vipers, how can ye escape the damnation of hell!" That is the loving, lowly Jesus when His anger is stirred.

§ 3. How His Anger Differs from Ours

Now from the anger of Jesus learn what anger should be in a good man's life. Much of our anger is weakness, not strength; peevishness, ill-temper, passion that we are too weak to control. And much of our anger is selfish because someone has hurt ourselves. And much of it is bitter and unforgiving. Now learn three things about Our Lord's anger.

(1) He was never angry at things done to Himself. Men might reject Him, despise Him, mock Him, spit on Him, nail Him in bitter agony to a cross. What did He say? "Father, forgive them, they don't know what they are doing." But let men pollute the house of God, or oppress the weak, or seduce a young girl into ruin and sin, then His anger would be fierce. No personal resentment. If a man smite Him on the cheek He would

turn the other. And he bids you do the same—if it be your own cheek. But if it be the cheek of some poor helpless one that is a very different matter.

(2) His anger is but the other side of His love. Because He loved the oppressed, He hated the oppressor. Because He loved the ruined girl, He would crush the seducer. Because He loved to see the people drawing near to God, His wrath fell on the hypocrites who were keeping them back.

(3) But especially learn this. That His wrath is always trembling on the brink of forgiveness. His anger is against wilful, deliberate, obstinate sin: against the hypocrite, the unloving, the obstinately unrepentant. But the first sign of sorrow would touch him into tenderness. To the tyrant and the hypocrite He speaks stern denunciation. To the sorrowful poor sinner at the first sign of penitence He tells stories like the Lost Sheep and the Prodigal Son.

Right anger is Divine. Wrong anger is hateful. We may be as angry as we like if we are angry like Jesus.

QUESTIONS FOR LESSON VI

What took Jesus to Jerusalem at this time?

Explain what the wrong was which made Him angry.

Why did not the people stop this wrong?

How does human anger differ from that of Jesus?

Now tell me carefully the three things that made His anger a fine thing.

LESSON VII

HOW JESUS CAME TO GALILEE

St. John III. 22-30, IV. 1-4

The pupil should have some idea of the sequence of events in Our Lord's life so far as we can get it. Impress on him that the two prominent periods are (1) The public ministry in Galilee, which lasted perhaps a year and a half to two years, and then (2) His going up to Jerusalem to die. We are now approaching the beginning of Galilean period. Notice this is the period which the three first Evangelists are mainly concerned with. All our lessons up to this are a sort of preface to this period. The Evangelists point back to these earlier days. They start out from them. But their main story begins here. And they indicate this by a bold landmark. "Now when John was delivered up Jesus came to Galilee preaching the Gospel of the Kingdom of God." (See Matthew iv. 12; Mark i. 14; Luke iv. 14, 31.) The teacher should get this clearly in his own mind and let pupil see that a crisis in Our Lord's life is now approaching. This lesson is to lead us into Galilee to the beginning of this public ministry.

58

§ 1. A Summer Tour in the Country

Last lesson left our Lord where? How long He stayed after Passover we do not know. Probably not long. The position in Jerusalem was difficult. The authorities were against Him. So He retired into the country with His disciples. And there for about six or eight months it would seem He moved about amongst the farmers and village people.

I sometimes think that perhaps He was deciding whether He would begin in Judea or in Galilee. At any rate we think of Him and his young comrades having a pleasant summer time in the country, tramping the country roads enjoying the brown hills and the sound of running streams, talking to the children, greeting passers-by on the road. They would meet perhaps a blind man or leper begging and heal him. The villagers would gather around in the evening and Jesus would tell them His delightful parable stories, lifting up their whole thoughts of life and of God's love. And I think they could not help loving Him and wishing to be like Him.

§ 2. John the Baptist Again

As we follow Him, suddenly, unexpectedly, we find ourselves in the neighbourhood of John the Baptist, still preaching and baptising. We thought his mission was over when he had baptised the Lord and pointed Him out as "The Lamb of God who taketh away the sins of the world." Well, it is soon going to be over, for King Herod and the Queen are angry with him and prison doors will soon open for him. Already his mission seems ending. No crowds now, no excitement about him. A few months ago he was at the height of popularity until he paused and pointed to One greater than himself. Gradually the crowds deserted him as the fame of Jesus increased. And John's disciples were vexed and jealous that their brave, silent master was being deserted. They can keep silent no longer. "Master, He to whom you bore witness beyond Jordan all men are following Him."

Now tell me John's beautiful answer, showing his big, unselfish heart. (*v.* 28, 29, 30). "It is all right," he says. "My day is over and I am satisfied, for remember what I told you, that I am nobody—only the messenger before the Christ. I am the humble friend of the Bridegroom rejoicing in His success. He must increase. I must decrease, this my joy therefore is fulfilled."

That is the last public word of his that is recorded. What do you think of it? A month later he was lying in the black dungeon of Machærus facing death. Herod and the wicked Queen have got him at last.

§ 3. When Galilean Ministry Began

There he lay, eating out his brave heart, till that horrible night when they cut off his head in the prison. But that story comes later on. Now I want you to see that just at this time comes a new crisis in the life of Our Lord. He is going out into the open to preach His Kingdom of God, to begin His public ministry in Galilee. (Read Matthew iv. 12; Mark i. 14; Luke iv. 14-31.) "When John was delivered up Jesus went north to Galilee preaching the Kingdom of God."

So we see Him and His young disciples leaving their summer tour and striking northward to Galilee. I think when they reached the Galilean border at the cross-roads, He bade good-bye to His companions. They had to go eastward, home to their fishing on the Lake of Galilee. He was going westward, perhaps home to Nazareth. But He probably told them that He was coming after them soon. And they waited. The waiting was good for them. I picture them daily at their fishing looking for His coming, talking and thinking of Him and learning to love Him more and miss His presence and so growing more fitted for their future with Him.

§ 4. The Nobleman's Son

And Jesus went away probably by Himself. We do not know what wonderful things may have happened on that journey. There was no one to tell. You know there is a great deal of His life left unrecorded. Don't you wish we knew it all?

St. John has just one little story of this time. Jesus had come to Cana—probably stayed with—whom do you think? What two people did He know there? One day while in Cana with Nathanael and the little bride a hurried message came. A nobleman or courtier of Herod had his little boy dying twenty miles away in Capernaum. He had ridden post-haste to Cana. "O Sir, come down ere my child die!" Jesus could not resist that. "Go thy way, thy son liveth." Next morning as his reeking horses were approaching Capernaum he met the joyful messenger from his wife. "Tell me," he asks, "when did he begin to recover?" "Yesterday, sir, at the seventh hour the fever left him." And the officer knew that at that very hour Jesus had said, "Thy son liveth." And he believed and all his house.

§ 5. How Jesus Came to His New Home

So Jesus had made another friend in Capernaum where he was going to live; where his young disciples were awaiting Him. Soon that family had a chance of thanking Him in person. For some days later Jesus is walking down the Lake road as it leaves Cana. An opening in the hills shows Him the Lake lying below and Chorazin and Bethsaida and Capernaum clustered on its western shore.

Probably some of His young fisher friends came to meet Him on the road and I can imagine the Capernaum people staring and gathering in groups as they watched their neighbours coming with the stranger Rabbi. And there is a tax-gatherer named Matthew, whom we shall hear of again perhaps, watching them from his office by the road. At any rate long afterwards he saw the importance of this coming. I want you to see how enthusiastically he wrote of it in his book. Read for me St. Matthew iv. 15, 16, telling of the great day when Jesus came to Galilee.

QUESTIONS FOR LESSON VII

This lesson begins an important new period in Our Lord's life. Explain.

What are the two great divisions of His life story?

Tell me about that pleasant summer tour in the country.

What stopped it?

Tell story of nobleman's son.

Make a word picture of the day when Jesus came to Capernaum.

THE GALILEAN MINISTRY

Emphasise here that we have come to a new period in our Lord's life—the Galilean ministry—a period of one to two years. Teach the Life in orderly sequence of events as they happened. So many people have in their minds just the disconnected happenings and teachings all mixed up. Our Lord's public life divides into two main parts: (1) "In the Highlands of Galilee" which occupies this whole volume. (2) "The Road to Jerusalem" which occupies the next volume. Get pupils to have a clear connected view of the whole life in order.

LESSON VIII

THE CALL OF THE FOUR FISHERMEN

St. Mark I. 14-21.

§ 1. Capernaum

Where did we leave Jesus in last lesson? Just arrived in Capernaum. In which province of Palestine? Yes, Galilee. Galilee was north, Judea was south. Pretty much like Scotland and England in old days. North was the highland province, like Scotland with its mountains and rivers and its brave highland people fighting for freedom. South was Judea, where, in the capital, Jerusalem, was a more civilised people but a more cowardly people submitting easily to the yoke of the Roman Empire. They rather looked down on the rough country folk of the north. But the brave men of the north rather looked down on them. There was jealousy and ill feeling between them.

Find Capernaum on a map. It is important in Jesus' life. Name the four towns where he lived. BETHLEHEM, where He was born; NAZARETH, where He was reared up; JERUSALEM, where He died; and CAPERNAUM, the centre of His Galilean ministry, "His own city" it is called, the scene of the most familiar stories in the gospels.

Look at the Lake of Galilee where so many things happened and then place Capernaum. Looking up from a boat on the Lake you would see on the hill the Roman castle which the people hated as the stronghold of their oppressors. But the centurion or captain there was a friendly man. "He loveth our nation and hath built us our synagogue." The rich people living on the hill. Down near the shore the shops and the fishermen and a crowd of boats with rough brown sails lying in the little harbour and outside. And the great white Roman roads ran near Capernaum. The Romans built them and took taxes to pay for them as travellers passed, and beside the town, just where it touches the Lake on one of these roads, was the Roman custom-house, where one Matthew, whom we know, sat at the receipt of custom.

Down near the strand is Simon Peter's house where he lives with his family and his wife's mother and his young brother, Andrew. This house is very important to us for in one of its rooms Jesus lodged whenever He was in Capernaum.

Now get Capernaum clearly in your mind and then read the well-known verse expressing Jesus' disappointment when He was going away from it later on. "Woe unto thee, Chorazin! Woe unto thee,

Bethsaida! And thou, Capernaum, exalted up to Heaven shall be cast down," etc. (Matthew xi. 21).

§ 2. The Call of the Four

Now you have some notion of His Galilean home when Jesus came to Capernaum. Here lived four young fishermen whom we have met before. You remember? (Lesson IV). Tell me of their first meeting with Jesus.

He was going to preach in Capernaum on the Sabbath. But I think that the week before He was going about with His young fisher friends. One night they had gone out fishing, a bad, stormy night, no fish to be got. Next morning Jesus out early on strand. He saw what? Torn nets, boats dirty, full of sand and the fishermen gone out of them mending their nets. Did He care for their disappointment? What did He bid them do? I suppose they did not see much good in trying again, but it was enough that He had said it. Now what happened? Nets bursting with multitude of fishes! What did Peter feel? Astonished—knew it was a miracle. They were amazed. They would be more amazed still some day. For as yet they had not begun to learn the greater miracle that He who had just filled their nets by the magic of His word was He who created the fishes of the sea and whatsoever walketh in the paths of the sea. It took some time before they learned that Jesus was God.

"Depart from me for I am a sinful man, O Lord!" Did he wish Jesus to go? No, but his own unworthiness oppresses him; he feels unfit to be with Him. Now tell me the Lord's reply. "Don't be afraid, from henceforth thou shalt catch men." Meaning of this? Yes. That was what the Lord was out for. Catching men and women and children into his lovely Kingdom of God to make them holy and happy and helpful to the world and then at death to move them to a higher Kingdom.

The Lord was on the look-out for helpers in His mission. He did not choose rabbis or rich or learned men. We do not know why. Somehow He saw in these young fishers the sort of men He wanted. And He was hinting here that He would call them away to be with Him and help Him to found His Kingdom. But this was no fit moment to say all this. The boats had to be cleaned. The great haul of fish had to be packed in boxes for the fish dealers in Tiberius and Jerusalem. So it was later, when the work was done, that Jesus said to Simon and Andrew, his brother, "Come ye after me and I will make you to become fishers of men." Then He said the same at the other boat to James and John who were with old Zebedee, their father, mending the nets.

Now they are not to be mere friends or disciples any longer. They are to go out as comrades and helpers in His great work. You might call this the beginning of the Christian church. Think how small—just five men walking up the strand in an obscure fishing village. But look at that church now spreading through the world. How is it like parable of the little seed growing into a great tree?

Don't forget that that Kingdom of God is still being built and every one of you is expected to help. How to begin? With yourself first. Get near to your Lord. Then do things to help. Get a comrade who does not go to church, or try to help someone going wrong. Jesus will call that building His Kingdom.

QUESTIONS FOR LESSON VIII

Describe and compare Galilee and Judea.

Try to picture Capernaum as Jesus knew it.

Tell of fishers' disappointment and the miracle.

How much did this Call of the Four mean?

Anything like it in our lives?

What four towns were prominent in life of Our Lord?

LESSON IX

THE FIRST SABBATH
IN CAPERNAUM

Read St. Mark I. 21 to end.

§ 1. Going to Church in Capernaum

Now comes a picture how the Lord spent His
Sabbaths. I think this was His first Sabbath in Capernaum, His first appearance in church, His first public
declaration in Galilee about His Kingdom of God.

Try to make the picture in your minds. Nine o'clock
in the morning usual hour of service. There are the
little crowds of village people on every path that led
to the Centurion's new white synagogue on the hill.
Rather like any country town to-day, except in the
bright-coloured dress of the people. The farmers and
fisherfolk coming with their families. Old Zebedee is
there, awkward in his Sabbath clothes, with his wife
and his big sons, James and John. Andrew is walking
with Peter and I think the Master is with them. And
Jairus, the ruler of the synagogue from the upper town,
and "the nobleman whose son was sick in Capernaum."

72

You remember? (Lesson VII). And surely with him the mother of that child to see and hear Him who had saved her boy. Streets crowded, bright with colour. Synagogue will be crowded. For they know the Stranger is sure to be in church and they expect the ruler of synagogue will ask Him to preach.

§ 2. The Sermon

Now they are in church. Scholars know the usual prayers of the synagogue. The First Prayer is said. The Second Prayer. The Jewish Creed. The six Benedictions. Then comes "the reading of the Church lessons." Here I see the Minister approaching the painted Ark and take out The Roll of the Law and The Roll of the Prophets. Then he looks at the Visitor in Peter's seat. "Sir, if you have any word of exhortation for the people, say on."

So Jesus rises in that crowded church. He begins by reading the Lesson from the Scriptures. Then He preached. I wish we had that sermon. Surely about the tender fatherhood of God and His love for the people. And about the Kingdom of God which He was founding on earth. We only know that the people were deeply interested and astonished "that He taught as one having authority, not as the Scribes."

§ 3. The Lunatic

But He never got that sermon finished. What happened? Wild disturbance in church, the women frightened, the people springing to their feet. A lunatic, a demoniac, a man with an evil spirit controlling his poor clouded brain. The excitement of the church and the preaching was too much for him. "Ea! Ea! what have we to do with thee, Jesus of Nazareth. I know thee, the Holy Son of God."

We do not quite understand. It suggests that evil spirits, as well as good, are around us. That an evil spirit had got hold of this poor creature and spoke through him. I do not know enough to explain. It is all puzzling. The calm, pitying eyes of Jesus are upon the poor madman. Then came His word of stern authority: "Hold thy peace! Come out of him!" And in a moment the poor man was healed. And the astonished people talked excitedly as they came home from church, saying—What did they say? (*v.* 27).

§ 4. Peter's Wife's Mother

But the Sabbath was not over yet. After service Jesus is going home to Peter's house and some others are invited to the "Sunday dinner." Who? (*v.* 29). Was Sunday dinner ready? What was wrong? I think Peter's wife's mother was the housekeeper. The "Great Fever," the scourge of that low lakeside, had stricken her and the whole house was upset. What did the Lord do? So those who had just come astonished from church were still more astonished. And two sufferers that day were happier for Jesus being there. Remember how Jesus' whole life was spent in making people happier and better.

§ 5. "At Even Ere the Sun Was Set"

And still the day is not over. Cannot you imagine the excitement of that little town, all day talking of the demoniac man and of the other miracle. And the hope in some of their hearts because Jesus was there and because they had many others sick and suffering. But they had to keep quiet at home until sunset which was the end of the Sabbath. Rules were very strict about this.

But as evening came the people in Peter's house could hear hurried footsteps and eager talking and the sounds of a gathering crowd and when they looked out they saw—what? "The whole town gathered together at the door." All over the strand, down to the waterside among the boats and the brown fishing nets drying on the shore were sick people on their mats and mothers with pining babies and a father leading his blind boy and affectionate poor people of all sorts longing to get their friends cured.

And Jesus looking from the door. Did He care? What sort of persons care most for others' troubles? The kindest people surely. They actually suffer in their sympathy. And surely Jesus would suffer much more. For Jesus is God. And nobody cares so deeply as God. All through the gospels that lesson is emphasised, the tender human sympathy of Jesus for individual suffering people. Is not it nice to think of it when you are suffering or sick? Here is a lovely precept for your life:

> "Kindness in another's trouble,
> Courage in your own."

That is what the Life of Jesus teaches.

But there is more than that. We are taught that He healed people at the cost of strain and loss to Himself. He was never sick so far as we know. His body was stored with perfect vigour and health. And of this He gave. "Somebody has touched me," He said, when a woman surreptitiously touched Him and was healed. "Somebody has touched me for I perceive that strength has gone out from me." That means that by giving of His own strength and health He gave strength and health to others. So St. Matthew in telling this same story gives a beautiful new meaning to the prophecy of Isaiah. "He hath borne our griefs and carried our sorrows." St. Matthew puts it thus: "He took our infirmities and bore our sickness." I think he meant that He took them on Himself and at His own cost healed them.

All that is exhausting. So the Lord must have been very tired as he lay down to sleep in Peter's room with the pleasant feeling that He had left so many happier and better. But He had a deeper need than bodily rest. So, "a great while before day," Peter hears him stealing out of the house to pray. He never could do without that, keeping in close communion with the Father. And He is very earnest in telling us to do the same. We should all be so much happier and better by keeping daily in touch with God.

QUESTIONS FOR LESSON IX

Picture the people going to church that morning.

What was their church service like?

What struck the people about the sermon?

Tell of the interruption.

What happened "at evening ere the sun was set"?

Why did they delay till evening?

Did the Lord sleep late next morning? Why?

LESSON X

REJECTED IN HIS HOME TOWN

Read St. Luke IV. 16-31;

Mark VI. 1-7.

I place this incident here as the most likely place. Some writers differ. Some think it was before He came to Capernaum. And St. Luke seems to agree with them. But the other evangelists do not. And Jesus' own words at Nazareth seem to settle the question, "Ye will say to me, Whatsoever things we have heard of in Capernaum do also here."

§ 1. Back Home

When Peter found the Lord that morning in prayer on the hillside we read that the Lord planned to go out on a tour of teaching in the villages. I place this visit to Nazareth in this tour though there are differences of opinion about it. The story is told as a separate incident without any mark of time. But it is hard to place it anywhere else. It cannot have been before He came to Capernaum. Why? (see *v.* 23).

So one evening in his wanderings He came to His old home, to "Nazareth where He had been brought up." How interesting to go back to the old home town; the village street where He had played with the other children; the old rabbi's school; the well, whence He had carried water for His mother and His carpenter's shop, now closed, and the old farmers He had worked for and the old friends who had been kind to Him and the fields and hills where He had roamed thinking out His great thoughts. And, above all, His mother, if she was still there in the little house by the carpenter's shop. I suppose old friends came to visit Him, who was now becoming famous, and acquaintances greeted Him respectfully in the street.

§ 2. In the Nazareth Synagogue

But we are chiefly interested now in His going to church on the Sabbath and what happened there. Just as in the Capernaum synagogue in last lesson we see the crowded church, the people so conscious of their Visitor, the ruler of the synagogue inviting Him to read the Lesson for the Day and preach. What a glorious lesson He had to read, what Isaiah had said long ago about the coming Messiah. Read it again. "The Spirit of the Lord is upon me," etc. (*vv.* 17-20). Then He sat down to preach. Very short sermon. But surely very startling. Repeat it. "This day is this Scripture fulfilled in your ears!"

Of course He said much more, but that was the subject. Perhaps as on a later day (Luke xxiv. 27) He interpreted to them in all the Scriptures the things concerning Himself. At any rate it was the most startling, exciting sermon ever heard in Nazareth. For it was a distinct assertion that He was the Messiah whom Israel had dreamed of through the centuries and a proclaiming of the sweet sympathy and graciousness of His Messianic mission. There were troubled people there and sinful and sorrowing people and people who had friends sick and suffering. How delightful, if it were true, to believe in this lovely message from God. Touched and impressed for the moment they wondered at the gracious words which proceeded out of His mouth.

But they could not believe it. It was too good to be true. Many feel like that to-day about God's tender fatherhood and His love and care and forgiveness. Too good to be true. Is that so? No. Nothing is too good to be true if it is told of God. For no one loves as God loves and when we get to Heaven we shall find that our wildest dreams of His goodness are far away below the truth.

They doubted. And then nasty, snobbish feelings arose in some of them because the preacher who claimed to be the Messiah was one of their old villagers, one of their old playmates, a common man like themselves or lower. Why some of them had hired Him to make chairs and cattle yokes a few years ago. Listen to them. "Is not this the carpenter, the Son of Mary? Are not His sisters with us plain people like ourselves?" And they were offended at Him.

It was an awful pity. But it was quite natural. Just what would happen in any country town to-day. So we must not blame them too much for that. I do not think Jesus did. Jesus was very reasonable, even with people's faults and weaknesses. He almost made an excuse for them. "A prophet has no honour in his own country," He said. Is not it lovely to think of Jesus understanding and making excuses for us, trying to make the best of us and see the best in us. He always did that. You remember His dying prayer on the Cross for the mocking multitude. "Father, forgive them, they are all excited now, they do not know what they are doing."

But still it was very wicked of them. For it was Jesus, so winsome and attractive and loving, who had preached to them, and I think true hearts could not help being attracted and loving Him. And they went beyond doubting. They got in a rage with Him. They seized Him and turned him out of the church and wanted to throw him off the precipice outside. No good people would do that, especially to one like Him.

So He had to go away saddened and disappointed, cut to the heart by His old friends and comrades just as He is often saddened and disappointed by us. But He is too noble to resent or bear grudges. He has no illusions as to the sort of people we are. Spite of it all He wants to bless us if we do not prevent Him, if we do not throw away our opportunity. Nazareth threw away its opportunity. Jesus had to go from them. And so far as we know Nazareth never saw Him again.

Do any of us behave like that toward Him now?

These people rejected Him because they were "used to Him," familiar with Him as one of themselves in the past years and therefore thought less of Him. Now that despised carpenter is known as the Son of God come down to earth—but His gospel is so familiar—we have got so "used to it" that we pay less attention to it. And so this touching message of God's tenderness and care, of the Christ dying for us on the Cross and planning His splendid adventure for us here and hereafter, is taken lightly and neglected and our dear Lord has to look down saddened and disappointed as in those far-off days in Nazareth. Can't we think it over for ourselves and pray for grace not to disappoint Him as they did?

§ 3. Because He Was God

One thing more. If you were in the Nazareth synagogue that day could you imagine anything more hopeless than that that young carpenter cast out by his people should go out to revolutionise the whole world—that He should be worshipped all over the earth to-day as God! That after two thousand years of men studying and testing and examining His life, He should be increasingly prayed to and adored. That the few words which He spake and the story of a few months of His life should be the greatest uplifting power that the world has ever known. That when they had crucified Him he should rise from the dead and bid men follow Him here in their life on earth and then follow Him into the great adventure of the Hereafter. How could such impossible things happen? What do you think? There is only one answer: Because He Was God.

QUESTIONS FOR LESSON X

Jesus went on a preaching tour. Why go to Nazareth?

Tell me the picture in your minds of His homecoming.

What is a synagogue?

Repeat the grand text of His sermon.

Why did the sermon startle them?

What else irritated them?

What in this story makes one feel that Jesus Was God?

LESSON XI

THE MAN WHO CAME THROUGH THE ROOF

Read St. Mark II. 1-13.

§ 1. *"Thy Sins Be Forgiven Thee!"*

We do not know any more about His tour through the villages. Only that after it He returned to Capernaum and it was noised abroad that "He was home" (*v.* 1, R.V. margin). You see, Capernaum is now regarded as "home."

So the crowds began to gather again. Crowds following. Diseased and deformed people brought to be healed. I am afraid they cared more for that than about hearing His gospel. This would disappoint Him, but He was very good to them and healed their sick.

Now I am thinking of a poor, lonely, paralysed man in his bed. I suspect he had brought the sickness on him through an evil life. And he was miserable about it all. Now a few old comrades rush into his room. "Jesus is home! He has cured worse cases than yours. He is most kindly when men are most miserable. Come on. Let us carry you. Who knows what may happen!" So these good fellows carry him off down the street, across the strand, to the house where Jesus was teaching. I think He was on verandah of house, preaching to crowd down in courtyard. Disappointment awaited these men. What? Crowds, crowds. They could not bring their friend even near the door. But they would not be put off. A bright thought occurred to them. What? "We cannot get near this house at all. Let us climb up on the roof next door. Then we can climb over the little parapet on to this roof; and then what?" Capital idea! Not the first time that fisherman had used his wits to get out of an awkward place!

Now look inside. Crowd in the courtyard. Jesus on verandah, seated. Suddenly noise above; light shining in; trap-door removed; tiles stripped off. And in a moment four brown sailor faces, smiling with delight at their clever idea; four cords tied in sailors' knots at corners of the mattress, and down, swinging through the roof, comes the poor frightened paralytic, down to the very feet of the Lord. I can imagine His good-natured smile at the kindly trick. He loved to see people trusting Him, and to see them determined not to be put off. Could He see into these men's hearts? (*v.* 2). Saw the love and the unselfishness, but, above all, the faith—*i.e.*, the *trust* in Him. He delights in being trusted.

But now see the man on ground looking up with dawning hope. What does he expect to hear Christ say? "Be healed." Does He say it? What does He say? (*v.* 5). Does not it seem strange to you? Do you think it disappointed the man? Not altogether, I think. Christ read his heart, as well as his friends' hearts. What did He read there? His illness probably result of his own sin; and, I think, in his lonely helplessness and depression he had become sorrowful and penitent. Is this only a guess of mine? How do I know it? Because I know Jesus would not have offered that precious gift of pardon to one careless and impenitent. He read the man's heart. And there is a great lesson here. He gave what He knew to be the greatest gift, the greatest need for man. We think sickness and pain the worst things. God says no—sin is the worst. To be pardoned and made holy is God's highest gift. And this poor man, I think, had begun dimly to see this.

But story not over yet. There were other hearts that He could read. (*v.* 3). Did they speak out their suspicions? But He knew them. These are the bigoted, uncharitable people who are always looking for faults. They were not touched by the pity on Christ's face, nor the trembling hope of the poor paralytic. The beauty of high character and the sorrows of troubled hearts are not nearly as prominent to this class of men as some fault that they can find out. And so, instead of thinking "He is kind and loving," they only think "He is blaspheming." (Read Mark ii. 7.) But were they not right about power of forgiving sins? Yes, though their feelings were uncharitable. None but God can forgive. Did Jesus then apologise for His words? Not a bit of it. He accepts their challenge at once. True, none else but God has power to forgive. "But I, the Son of Man, have power." Therefore, what follows? Tell me proof

He gave them. And the man took up his bed—*i.e.*, mat or mattress. I hope you did not think it a big four-post bedstead! What impression made on the people?

§ 2. Lessons of the Story

Now what do you think we can learn from this story? Think it out yourselves.

(1) The tender kindliness of Jesus smiling with amused pleasure at the friendship and the clever trick of these good fellows and then giving His whole attention to that poor man as if no one else in the world wanted Him. I like to think of Jesus being amused. God made smiles and laughter and I am sure there are smiles and laughter and humour in heaven. And we believe Jesus gives each of us as close attention when we come as if no one else existed.

(2) Jesus dealt with the man's soul first. We would think the first thing was to heal his body. But Jesus knew his misery and remorse for his sin. And in any case He thought it more important to touch his soul by teaching God's love and the forgiveness of sin. We say, It is a blessed thing to bring happiness and comfort. Yes, says Jesus, but it is a more blessed thing to bring them God. We say, It is a great thing to build good healthy houses in the slums. Yes, says Jesus, but it is still greater to build noble souls to live in them.

(3) His anger at the bitterness and unloving hearts of the Pharisees who were vexed. To Him the greatest sin is the sin of an unloving heart.

QUESTIONS FOR LESSON XI

Tell briefly of man coming through the roof.

Two things were troubling him.

Which did Jesus deal with first? How?

And why?

Who objected and why?

How did He answer them?

What is the worst sin in His sight?

LESSON XII

ST. MATTHEW AND HIS BANQUET

Read Matthew IX. 9-14; Mark II. 14-22;

Luke V. 24-39.

§ 1. The Call of St. Matthew

One day we are told "Jesus was teaching by the shore and as He returned He saw Levi, the son of Alphæus, sitting at the receipt of custom and He said unto Him, Follow Me, and he arose and followed Him."

Rather a puzzling story. Why? (1) That Jesus should call a man of this class to be one of His helpers. Publican means tax-collector. Of course every government must collect taxes to carry on its work. We do not much object to tax-collectors. But suppose we were conquered by Germany or some other nation and felt the oppression sorely and that some of our own people offered to go and collect the taxes from their countrymen to help the oppressing nation. Would a good patriot Jew do it? Only a lower type who would do anything for money.

But worse than this. The taxes were farmed out to the collector. He paid a large sum to government for the taxes of a district and then wrung more out of the people for his profit and used the power of the oppressing Roman nation to force people to pay. Should we like these men? They were rich, but despised and hated. No decent Jew would speak to them.

(2) But it looks also strange that Jesus should suddenly call any man, especially one of this class and that such a man should promptly respond. For Jesus was very particular about the men He chose as Apostles and turned down several men who offered. There was that Scribe who offered himself (Matthew viii. 19). "I will follow thee whithersoever thou goest." One would think an honoured Scribe would be a valuable helper. And the rich young man who went away sorrowful (Luke xviii. 23). Jesus, beholding him, loved him. But He put a severe test on him. "Sell all that thou hast and give to the poor." So the rich young man dropped out. The Lord certainly did not choose His Apostles lightly. Why then this publican? Can you guess the answer?

§ 2. Preparation for the Call

I am sure He did not call Matthew till he was fit to be called. There must have been much previous intercourse between them. I notice that he is called the son of Alphæus. And three other Apostles were sons of Alphæus, probably the same man. If so, Matthew was their brother though they would be ashamed to acknowledge him, and probably also a family connection of Jesus. It is not unlikely that he knew Jesus in boyhood and lost sight of Him when he disgraced his family by becoming a publican, and that Jesus renewed the acquaintance when He found him in the Capernaum custom house.

Matthew could not help liking Him, the only one of his connections who would speak to him at all. I think he was always ashamed of his trade when Jesus came into his office. And the more he saw of Jesus the more ashamed he grew and the more desirous to win Jesus' approval. I imagine the soul of the man growing through the silent influence of Jesus. Jesus used to preach on the shore near his office and I think I can see him often listening on the outskirts of the crowd and wishing to be better and perhaps sometimes telling Jesus of his thoughts.

I am only guessing. But I am quite sure that something like this happened, else Jesus would never have appointed him. So one day Jesus came to the office and called him and Matthew, in his surprise and delight, immediately "left all and followed Him." He was a penitent man, ashamed of his old life. Probably because of him Jesus was called by his enemies "a friend of publicans," and poor Matthew never forgot it and humbly writes himself down in his own gospel as "Matthew the publican" (Matthew x. 3). Now are you surprised at Jesus choosing him?

§ 3. Eating with Publicans and Sinners

Then Matthew did rather a brave thing. He gave a

great farewell dinner to the staff in his office and to all the publicans around to celebrate this change in his life. Why was it brave? He was not ashamed to tell his comrades that he was a converted man and that the holy Jesus meant so much to him. They might sneer at this, but his religion made him brave enough to risk it. And it did not make him feel too conceited and superior to associate with his old comrades whom all others would be ashamed of. Don't you think Matthew must have been rather a fine type of man in spite of his ugly trade?

He had a large costly house, for "multitudes" came to his banquet (Luke v. 29). Evidently he had riches and gave it all up to follow in poverty a Master who had nothing and not even where to lay His head (Matthew viii. 20). And I think he must have known the heart of Jesus well, else he would not have dared invite Him to dine with his despised comrades. I am sure they had a pleasant dinner and felt proud of being there. And I am sure Jesus did not despise them or treat them with patronising condescension that might hurt. He treated every man respectfully. For every man is of infinite value in the sight of God. And I am sure every man at Matthew's feast that day felt himself a better man for having been there with Jesus.

When you think of this, always remember that Jesus was God and all His kindly relations with men reveal to us what the heart of God is like. That is what draws us to Him. We do not know if any were definitely converted at that dinner, but one likes to see in the after days how often "the publicans and sinners drew near to Him to hear Him." And we shall hear later of another rich publican down at Jericho in the custom house who probably heard all about this dinner and the attitude of Jesus and climbed up into a tree to get a sight of Him who was kindly and respectful even to publicans and sinners. Jesus did not make light of their faults and sins. But He had the habit of always looking for the good in men rather than the evil and by means of that little good in them He would attract them to Himself. Why, do you think, are many not attracted to Jesus? Just because they do not know Him. I think if He were known as He really is and as those poor publicans knew Him, He would draw all men unto Him.

§ 4. Why Jesus Liked Being with Them

Of course the Scribes and Pharisees and respectable people were fiercely angry. Next day they attacked the disciples. What did they ask? "Why eateth your Master with publicans and sinners?" It seemed to them a most shameful thing, degrading to Jesus. Why should He keep such company? What did Jesus reply? (Matthew ix. 12). What did He mean? That the physician likes to go to the people that want him most. These poor despised sinners have no one to warn or comfort or help them. You contented people don't want me. They are sick in their souls and they often feel it. And then they need some one like me. And I like to be with them. They are God's poor sinful children astray in the woods and I want to show them the path home.

A year later as He went up to Jerusalem to die, a

similar thing happened as He passed through Jericho. There another rich publican sought Him and gave a dinner in His honour and the Jericho people were similarly angry with Him. And there, to explain the tender fatherhood of God over such poor sinners, He told them the three loveliest stories in the whole gospels. What were they? (Luke xv.)

QUESTIONS FOR LESSON XII

Explain Jewish contempt for publicans.

Two things seem strange in this call of St. Matthew. What would explain them?

What offended the Pharisees?

Another publican later on with whom a similar thing happened. Who?

In this latter case He gives a beautiful answer.

THE BUSY STRENUOUS LIFE OF JESUS

St. Mark IV and V.

These are too long to read. Let the class keep Bible open as they follow the lesson.

Teacher say to class: Not quite satisfied with teaching up to this for (1st) we haven't yet touched the central point of subject: the teaching of the Kingdom of God which meant so much to Jesus and ought to have been at the back of our thoughts all along—but we are not quite ready for this yet.

And (2nd) we seem rather thinking of Jesus as dealing with separate individual cases, not realising the vast crowds always about Him and the busy, strenuous life which He lived. This we are now to deal with.

§ 1. Multitudes

Making pictures in our mind of Jesus in Galilee we must always keep the multitudes around Him—crowds of simple, earnest people—listening, liking, applauding.

Evidently he was immensely popular. We read: "The multitudes thronged Him." "All men are seeking Thee." "All the city was gathered together at the door." "They came to Him from every quarter." "The people hung on Him—listening." "His mother and brethren could not come at Him—for the crowds." Crowds, enthusiastic crowds, pressing on Him all the time. "So many coming and going there was no leisure so much as to eat." And these were not merely curious crowds but crowds that were fond of Him.

And this not merely in the early Galilee days. Right to the end He was the popular hero. The people championed Him. He was always safe when they were about. When His enemies would seize Him "they feared the people," they said. "Not on the Feast Day—lest there be an uproar of the people." They had to get Judas to betray Him "in the absence of the multitude." They had to arrest Him at night when the people were in bed. And even if a little priest-ridden crowd yelled "Crucify Him" at His trial, the big crowds at Calvary, "when they saw what was done, beat their breasts and returned."

They couldn't help liking Him, He was so human, so friendly, so pleasant, and He was one of themselves, a man of the people, who could sympathise with them as no one else could. No man in those crowds was poorer or had worked harder than He. And He had a genius for looking for the best in men though He knew the worst. That always draws out the best in men. Now remember that this was God in human form who so attracted them. Maybe God would attract us all if we got to know Him as they did.

§ 2. A Specimen Day

Now to find out about His strenuous life. Pick out one day as a specimen. Keep Bibles open at St. Mark iv. and v. The time is a spring morning about March, A.D. 28. The scene opens (ch. iv. 1-10) with a very great multitude pressing on Him so that He had to push off from the shore in His boat to teach them. He is telling the parable of The Sower, and the three sorts of ground—the stony, the thorny, and the good soil—the human hearts in which He Himself was sowing the seed of the Kingdom. It was hard work teaching. They were stupid people. Not even His close disciples understood at first. We shall discuss this parable later on, we only mention it now.

Next we find Him "when He was alone," probably after the mid-day dinner, expounding this parable to his disciples (*vv.* 10-20). St. Matthew suggests another great crowd in the afternoon—probably that was the time of the kindred parables of the lamp and the mustard seed and the grain growing secretly. Probably there were questions asked and answered and miracles of healing as He moved amongst the people. Evidently there was excitement in the air that day. We find men crowding forward offering to be His helpers. A scribe said: "I will follow Thee wherever Thou goest." Another said: "I will follow You when my father has died." He tested and turned them down. They were not sufficiently in earnest. So passed that long, hot afternoon.

§ 3. Evening

Now it was late evening and He was growing tired (*vv.* 25-31). There had been a good deal of strain that day. He looked on the cool waters of the lake. "Bring round the boat, He said, let us go to the other side, so they took Him as He was into the boat and the disciples followed with Him." Probably they didn't like the look of the sky as they started but the Master wished it and He was tired. It was a long sail of seven miles in the teeth of the wind. Lying in the stern-sheets, very weary, He soon fell asleep, and as He slept the spray was wetting Him and the storm was rising and clouds were gathering black over the farther shore.

Soon a fierce storm broke and the strong fishing smack was tossing like a paper boat and they had no time to run for shelter. They were in serious peril. Never before had they to cry to a land's man as the boat began to sink: "Lord, save us, we perish!" Already they were learning to turn to Him in every trouble. They were learning their life lesson. Then He awoke and rebuked the winds and said unto the sea: "Peace, be still," and there was a great calm and the men marvelled. "What manner of man was this that even the winds and sea obeyed Him!"

§ 4. The Madman of Gadara

That tempest during the night had driven the boat to the southern end of the lake. The land of the half-heathen Gadarenes (ch. v. 1-20). In the morning twilight they landed near the old cemetery, following their Master with solemn awe. Immediately a new fright is on them. Horrible cries amongst the rocks and graves and a big murderous lunatic, stark naked, clashing his broken chains, was charging down on them. They recognise him at once as the "madman of Gadara," the terror of the whole countryside, a man with an unclean spirit, who had his dwelling in the tombs and no man could any more bind him, no not with chains, because the chains had been rent asunder by him, and no man had any strength to tame him. And always night and day in the tombs and in the mountains he was crying out and cutting himself with stones.

Suddenly the furious creature stopped when he saw Jesus and threw himself at His feet; perhaps some momentary glimpse of sanity drove him there for protection. But it passed in a moment. Some evil spirit power regained possession of his mind. "What have I to do with Thee, Jesus, Thou son of the Most High! I adjure Thee by God torment me not!"

Why do you think Jesus asked his name? To make him pull himself together and to recollect himself. In vain. "My name is Legion for we are many." The strong man armed was keeping his palace. But a stronger than he had come on him and overcame him. "Come out of the man, thou unclean spirit," and in a moment the poor demented creature had come to himself, become his own man again, standing in a sane world with a brotherly hand upon his shoulder. Men had tried man's way of taming him, Jesus had tried God's.

§ 5. Back to Capernaum

Now they are sailing back to Capernaum again; an excited crowd is awaiting Him on the landing stage. There is a man pressing through the crowd to find Him. A man who had been all night waiting. "Oh, Master, my little daughter! She is at the point of death. But come and lay Thy hand upon her and she shall live!" Jesus knew him, Jairus the ruler of the synagogue, and probably knew the child. He started to go with him.

But something happened on the way which made them pause in spite of Jairus' impatience. World very full of trouble. When you try to relieve one case, you find many more. Poor woman had been ill since the very year that Jairus' daughter was born. How do you know? Picture the scene carefully, and point out—(1) That Jesus felt the power go out of Him, and therefore probably had to perform His miracles of healing at loss and strain to Himself (see last Lesson). (2) That it has a spiritual meaning. Crowd in church to-day; all seem thronging and pressing about Christ. But do all *touch* Him like this woman, so as to get power and healing from Him? No; only those who, with earnestness and trust, reach out to Him. (3) That Christ accepts very stupid, ignorant faith. She thought superstitiously that the power might be in His clothes. Yet He did not reject her, but taught her to know Him better. Tell story of "Daft Jamie," a poor, half-idiot boy in Scotland, too stupid to be let go to Holy Communion. But he longed to go, and at last the kind minister allowed him. Poor boy was full of joy and excitement all day. "Oh, I hae seen the bonnie Man!" Next morning he was found dead in his bed. In the night-time he had passed away in his joy, and gone to see "the bonnie Man" for ever and ever.

Poor Jairus! Can't you imagine his agony of mind at this delay, and how he would turn away from the woman to watch with feverish eagerness the windows of his house on the hillside? "Oh! my little girl will die before He comes!" And even as he thinks of it, he hears galloping hoofs, and sees his servant approach. One glance at the man's face is enough. "Too late! Your little daughter is dead. No use troubling the Rabbi now!" Poor Jairus! But Jesus' ear was quick to hear that message, and his eye meets the poor father's glance. "Don't be frightened; only trust me still!" Hard to trust now. Christ had healed sickness, but never raised the dead before. Half-frightened, half-hoping, the poor father went on. Then, with father, and mother, and three disciples (which?), He goes into the little girl's shaded room, where she lay, all silent and still, in her little bed, with the curtains drawn tight around it. What was the matter? Dead? What did he call it? Why? Because since His coming, death is softened into sleep for all who love Him. They shall waken when He comes back. So Christians try to put away ugly old name (John xi. 11; 1 Thessalonians iv. 14), and put the word "sleeps," on their tombs, instead of "death." "She only sleeps," said the Lord, and went to awake her. How? By strenuous, repeated effort, like Elisha? (2 Kings iv. 34). By praying, like Peter, that God would raise her? (Acts ix. 40, 41). No. In calm, quiet power, just touched her hand and wakened her—perhaps in the very words by which her mother wakened her every morning, "Wake up, my little girl." "My little girl." He was so fond of these pet expressions of affection. Twice already in this chapter. (*vv.* 2, 22). "Cheer up, my son—my daughter." And now, "My little girl." The words must have stuck in Peter's memory always; and long years afterwards, when telling the story to St. Mark, he remembered the very word *Talitha*, the diminutive of endearment in the popular language used by the Lord. *Talitha cumi* (Mark v. 41).

From this one day you can judge how strenuous His life was. It was a tired, happy Jesus that laid down in Peter's little room that night; surely with the pleasant thought of the poor lunatic and the little girl's mother, and all the poor sufferers that He had made happy that day. That is what makes the happiness of God. That is the God with whom we have to do with in the struggle of life, in its pain and sorrow, in the hour of death and in the day of judgment. Thanks be to God.

QUESTIONS FOR LESSON XIII

Show the great popularity of Jesus in these early Galilean days.

Did they keep on caring right to the end? Prove this.

Now trace for me this specimen strenuous day: Morning, afternoon, evening, midnight, and next morning.

HOW TO KEEP SUNDAY

St. Matthew XII. to v. 38.

The chief lesson to be learned to-day is the way to think of our Sundays. Although the Jewish Sabbath does not quite correspond to the Christian Sunday, yet our Lord's teaching about the right spirit of keeping the Sabbath expresses exactly the way in which we should think of Sunday. But there is a further lesson too. The sin of an unloving heart. This lesson marks the beginning of troubles in the Lord's life. The bigoted Jerusalem Jews had come down. They were angry at His mixing with publicans and sinners and choosing a publican as one of His band. Now they were spiteful about the Sabbath. The unloving heart spoils happiness everywhere. Never again now to the close of His life shall He have back again those happy first days in Capernaum.

§ 1. Going to Church through the Fields

The Lord Jesus was very careful about attending the public worship of the church. Even though the clergy were often bad, and careless, and hypocritical, yet the church was the church, and no fault in the individual

103

minister could excuse any man for neglecting his oppor-
tunities of the regular worship of God.

Remember this when you grow up. You may move
to a parish where, for some reason, you may not be
attracted by the clergyman. That sometimes may
happen through the fault of the clergyman. It very
much oftener happens through people unreasonably
taking up prejudices, and not trying to think the best
and make the best of him. It is so easy to be sharp and
censorious towards one's pastor, easy to misunderstand
a man, and put unfair constructions on some word, or
act, or manner. But the important lesson here is that
the Jewish clergy, and scribes, and teachers as a body
were *really* bad, cruel, and hypocritical, and hostile to
Christ; and yet He and His disciples went regularly to
church to be ministered to by these men. Even after the
chief priests had crucified Him, still the Apostles went
regularly to the temple worship, and kept the regular
hours of prayer. We hear of them at worship at the third
hour, the sixth hour, the ninth hour. They had their
temple prayer-book and their synagogue prayer-book,
with fixed services of prayers, and psalms, and lessons
from the Scripture; and no fault in the minister could
spoil those for them.

Going to church, did they go by the road or through
the fields? What happened on the way? Just think of
the poverty of Jesus when His disciples were so hungry
going through the fields. Was He Himself hungry? Be
sure He did not eat food if there was not enough for
them. Besides, by comparing His case with that of David
(*v.* 3), He seems to suggest that "He was hungered, as

well as they that were with Him." Did you ever pluck ripe wheat-ears, and rub them on your hands? Did it seem like work, like Sabbath-breaking? Yet some silly people in our Lord's day thought so. Straight behind the disciples were the spiteful Pharisees from Jerusalem, spying on them. They were glad to see them break one of their wretched little Sabbath rules, which said that to pluck an ear of corn was to reap, to rub it was to thresh; and so, they said, the disciples were reaping and threshing on the Sabbath Day! What a silly, stupid thing to say. Had God given an order against reaping and threshing on the Sabbath? Why? In order that the poor, tired workers should be happy and restful, and that no cruel master should work them on the day of rest. It was a kindly, loving order of God. Was it kindly and loving when enforced by these Pharisees? What should they have rather done? Pitied the men for being hungry, and asked them to come and eat with them. Ah! that was not their way of showing religion. That was Christ's way. They would much rather try to find fault, and pretend it was for the sake of religion.

What two examples does Jesus quote? First means that any mere *ceremonial* law about worship must give place to urgent bodily necessity. The great law of Right and Wrong must not be broken for any necessity. It is better to die than to do wrong. But a mere rule about worship is on a different level. But what means second example? What has it to do with the case? (See *vv.* 6-8). "I am God, where I stand is a Temple—is holy ground. These poor followers of mine, acting in my service, are as guiltless as the priests in the Temple on the Sabbath.

And if ye were kind and merciful men, ye would not have condemned the guiltless."

§ 2. In Church

So they went on to church. And the Pharisees went too, and sat in their places at the top, and watched with scowling faces as Jesus entered with His disciples. What had these Pharisees gone to church for? To pray to be made loving, and kind, and good? Not a bit of it. (See Mark iii. 2.) To watch Him. What wicked, spiteful men! Did not like Christ, because He was so real and true; He hated cant and hypocrisy, and sternly rebuked them for it, even before the people. So they lay in wait, and set traps for Him. I suspect this whole affair in the synagogue was a trap laid by them; that they had put that man there to induce Jesus to break their rules, and then watched to try if they could catch Him. Reading the accounts in the different gospels leaves that impression.

What ailed the man? (v. 10). One of the old lost gospels says he was a stone-mason, and had told the Lord that he could not earn bread for his family. Picture—village church—man on seat—arm hanging dead—his eager eyes fixed on Jesus. Jesus' pitying eyes on him. Now see the Pharisees whispering and watching. Oh, this wicked Sabbath-breaker! going to heal a man on Sabbath! Hear them call out to stop Him. "Is it lawful to heal," etc. (v. 10). His reply (Mark iii. 4). Is it better on Sabbath to do *good*, as I am doing, or to do *harm* by neglecting to relieve misery? Then He appeals to their compassion. How? (*v.* 11). Yes. "You surely would pull out the sheep. Would you do less for a poor human being? Wherefore it is lawful to do good on the Sabbath Day." All this time the poor man waiting with his dead arm by his side. What next? Could he stretch it forth? Was it not dead? Yes; but when Christ told him, the poor fellow tried to do it, and *with the effort to obey came the power.* So with us—weak, powerless—can't love God, can't conquer sin, can't be truly faithful. But let us say, "Lord, I can't love Thee much; I can't serve Thee as I should; I can't be good as I ought; but, Lord, I'll try!" and *with the effort to obey will come the power.*

Do you think the poor stone-mason was glad? And the people? And the Lord? Were the Pharisees? What did they do? Went out to make plans against Him, and so went on and on in this wicked spitefulness, till they brought the Lord at last to the Cross on Calvary.

§ 3. How To Think of Sunday

Was it right for the Pharisees to be careful about keeping Sabbath? Yes; but they were so silly about it, and so spiteful, they forgot God's loving purpose for it. They would make Sabbath a torment.

Did God give Sabbath to be a torment to people? What does the Lord tell the Pharisees about it? (Mark ii. 27). *Made for man, i.e.,* for man's blessing and happiness. Does God like to see happy faces on Sunday? Like to see us out in fresh air, enjoying this beautiful world? Yes, we are His children, and He made Sunday for our happiness, and recreation, and rest. No

Latin, or sums, or hard school lessons to-day for boys and girls. No work for tired men and women. What an awful world if no Sundays! God says to us every Saturday night, "Come ye apart and rest awhile. I want you to rest and be happy." "This is the day that the Lord hath made: let us rejoice and be glad in it." Is it not good of our Father in Heaven? What a shame to make it gloomy!

But something else needed besides rest. We have another part of us besides bodies. Souls. And God, who wants us to be happy, knows that a good, noble, beautiful life will best make us so. He says, "If My children only think of rest and amusement, they may forget about goodness and about My love for them, and so lose their highest happiness. The busy men and women may forget Me in the hurry of their work; so I want to remind them about Me every Sunday, and keep them near to me." Emphasise the two sides. (1) The rest and recreation for the body. (2) Helps and reminders for the soul. And all *for the purpose of our good*, to make us happy, and holy, and loving to God and man.

Now, the Pharisees forgot the happy meaning of Sabbath. Thought of as a taskmaster's order to his slaves: "Don't do this, don't do that on Sabbath, or else I will punish you." Our Lord was vexed at the way they were spoiling God's beautiful gift, and so He often, in order to teach them, intentionally broke through their silly rules, intentionally worked miracles on Sabbath—broke the Sabbath, they would say. It is a great loss and pity when boys and girls and men and women are taught to think of Sunday as the Pharisees did. As if God's purpose were to worry and restrict you, and forbid all the things you like, and make you feel that it is only unpleasant things that are religious. I am so afraid of your taking up the silly notion that Sunday is an irksome thing, and that it would be nicer for every one to be free to do what he liked.

§ 4. *Danger of Losing Sunday*

If you examine the different passages in the Bible, even about the old Jewish Sabbath, you will find that the two chief directions about it were:

1. "Thou shalt rest from thy work on this day."

2. "Thou shalt *rejoice* and *be glad* in it."

True, they were not allowed to do as they pleased about it. Many would prefer working and making their servants work; many cried, When will the Sabbath be gone? that they might buy and sell, and get gain (Amos viii. 5, etc.), and wring the last drops of sweat out of those who served them. But God allowed no evasion—"Thou shalt do no manner of work, . . . nor thy manservant, nor thy maidservant, nor thy cattle," etc. Can't you see what a kindly rule it was—how many a poor Jewish labourer, with weary limbs and aching head, learned to thank God, and rejoice in His rest, that no greedy, tyrannous master could deprive him of.

And can't you see what a great and blessed thing it is still, even for this lower advantage of bodily rest—how, in the terrible strain and competition of these days, we ought to thank God for His law of Sunday. What fools

109

people are when they talk of Sunday as a restriction placed on them. I wonder how children would like doing school work just the same Sunday and week-day. Well, men and women will come to have to do their work every day alike if Sunday is lost to them. They ought to guard it rather as a precious heritage. I see great danger of losing it altogether in these days. It is a good thing to get people out into the country, and let them enjoy nature. But I see more and more, under the excuse of this, how men are being deprived of their Sunday rest. I see shops getting to be opened more than they used. I know men that do not get one Sunday off work in a year. I see tram-drivers and railway-men moving into slavery where seven days' work will be exacted for six days' pay. And, in the fear of all this, we want you young people to see God's good purpose in the Day of Rest, and fight hard that your country should not lose it.

I need not remind you that there is even a more important thing than bodily rest—that our lives should be made noble, and peaceful, and true, and good. For this we must have religion. For religion we must have our Sundays.

Remember, then, that the Sabbath was made for man—for man's body, his soul, his happiness, his peace—and never think of Sunday except as a great blessing from God.

So these *unloving* people spoiled the happiness of Jesus and so began the cruel road that was at last to lead Him to Calvary.

LESSON XV

THE KINGDOM OF GOD

St. Mark I. 14-16 and IV. 26-33.

The object of the teacher in this Lesson should be to leave a clear, definite impression as to the meaning of "the Kingdom of God." It is most important to get true views about this—to get rid of the selfish thought that Christ lived and died only that I, and certain who believe as I do, should go to Heaven when we die. Teach them of Christ's beautiful ideal—try to rouse their enthusiasm for it—to send them out with an impression of what Christ intended the Church to be. Probably the Lesson here is too long. But with deep, prayerful study of the subject, the teacher who is in earnest can leave the desired impression with fewer words.

§ 1. His Vision of the Future

(1) THE KINGDOM OF GOD. I want to start with a question which will need all your thinking to answer. What was the favourite, the constant, subject of our Lord's preaching? Almost all teachers who are capable of excitement and enthusiasm about their work, have

111

some special pet subject—Temperance or Missions, or Housing of Poor, etc., about which they get most enthusiastic, always wanting to talk about it, always wanting to rouse us about it; every conversation, every sermon of theirs will somehow lead up to it. People say—Well, that man has Temperance, Missions, etc., on the brain. He can't talk of anything else!

We may reverently say our Lord, too, had one pet subject, one pet enthusiasm, the centre of all His teaching. Every sermon, every parable, referred to it. His whole life was the picture, the model, the revelation of it. It was the vision that filled up all His hopes, all His outlook into the future. What was it? Think. Try again. His very first sermon in these portions that you have read was about it. What was it? Yes. THE KINGDOM OF GOD. In Concordance you find it nearly 100 times mentioned: *e.g.*, Mark i. 15; Luke iv. 43; viii., ix. 1, etc., etc.

Again, see parables—Kingdom of God like leaven—hid treasure—seed sown in a field, etc., etc. Main thought in them is the Kingdom of God. (Take trouble to learn and to impress on class that the Divine Reformer, like all the greatest of human reformers, was pre-eminently possessed with one great idea, and that idea was the Kingdom of God.)

§ 2. *What Did He Mean?*

(2) WHAT DID HE MEAN BY IT? You say He meant Heaven—a happy land to go to when we die? No, He did not. Most certainly He did not. At least, going to

Heaven was only a part—the far-off part—of His plan. Whatever He meant, it was clearly something that first of all concerned this earth, that had to begin, and grow, and spread for a blessing on earth.

Remember parables about it. What was it like? Little mustard seed growing to a great tree—little bit of leaven spreading through a lot of flour—a little corn of wheat springing up, first the blade, then the ear, etc. Would that mean Heaven? No. It was a little something that He was planting in the world that should spread and grow till it grew to be a great thing—till it leavened all around it. Can you not yet guess what He meant?

Well, let me try to picture what I think was the vision rising in His mind when He thought with glad hope and enthusiasm about the success of His plan. I can imagine that I see it before me. Try and make the picture in your minds as I go on. He sees before Him a sweet, fair vision—a band of boys and girls, and men and women, of true, noble, generous, Christ-like hearts; the sort of people that you can't help loving and admiring; the sort of people that make life so happy and lovely for all around them. Do you know any person like that? It is a small band at first—small, like a grain of mustard seed—only about twenty or thirty, but growing, growing, as the ages go on, till it overspreads the face of the earth. He sees in the vision how everything bad and miserable vanishes before them—all greediness, and lying, and bullying, and spite, and drunkenness, and impurity—all selfishness and cruelty—all poverty, and misery, and pain. They are such brave, generous boys, such tender, unselfish girls—such noble, self-sacrificing

113

men and women, in some degree like the Lord Himself. They care for nothing but what is good and true. They fear nothing but grieving their Lord. Their chief thought is the service of the Kingdom—making all life around them happy, and holy, and beautiful. Would not it be lovely to see a great growing band like that, increasing every day? Would not they make this a happy, holy, beautiful world? Would not they watch over the sick? help the drunkard? and comfort the sorrowful? Do you think the mean, sneaking sort of boys would dare to be mean and sneaking? Would not the spiteful and untruthful, and selfish girls be utterly ashamed of themselves? Would not many people want to join the ranks of this Kingdom of God, if they saw it so grand, so beautiful, spreading over the earth? Well, that is, I think, the vision of our Lord. That is what He meant by the Kingdom of God. Which should begin where? On earth. And go on whither? To heaven.

For years He had brooded on that vision on the hills of Nazareth. It grew as He made chairs and cattle-yokes for the people. Was it not a lovely vision! If that vision should materialise earth would be singing unto the Lord a new song, and when their life here was over, the members of His kingdom should pass within the Veil to be a Kingdom of God in the Unseen Land. Now do you understand what He wanted to plant on this earth? His Kingdom of God.

§ 3. "As It Is in Heaven"

Was it a mere dreamer's vision? Does it exist

anywhere? See what He bids us pray for in His prayer of the Kingdom:

THY KINGDOM COME

THY WILL BE DONE

ON EARTH *as it is in heaven.*

Therefore that Kingdom exists somewhere now. Where? He has brought His picture of it from the Home Above, the picture of His Kingdom *as it already exists in Heaven.* He was only founding a colony on earth of the already existing Kingdom in Heaven. That Kingdom there was behind the enterprise, throwing out its new colony into a new region as the great Roman Empire used to do. Therefore the whole Spiritual Universe, the God of that Universe, the Angels and Archangels and all the Company of Heaven are responsible for it. So one day in spite of all drawbacks it must inevitably succeed.

Sometimes people lose heart and think that religion is failing, that the Kingdom is set back, but it is like when on the sea-shore you watch the tide now advancing a little, now receding. But always inevitably *the tide comes in!* So with the Kingdom. God is behind it. The tide is coming in. One day in spite of all reverses, "The Kingdom of this world shall become the Kingdom of the Lord and of His Christ and He shall reign for ever and ever."

§ 4. *The Kingdom and the Church*

Where is that Kingdom to be found on earth to-day? It is represented by the church, the great Church of God throughout the world. Is it satisfactory, like the Kingdom above? No, for it has had to be planted amongst faulty, imperfect people down here. Is it one unbroken Kingdom as He intended? No, through fault and peevishness of men it is divided up into different bodies who refuse to worship together. Are all the members earnest about it? No. That is what spoils it and disappoints our Lord. That is what brings shame upon His Church.

The Kingdom of God is the Church. But all its members are not in earnest now, as they were then. Can't you fancy how disappointed the Lord is as He looks upon the careless boys and girls and men and women, who don't care at all to do the blessed work of His Kingdom. What a pain to His heart. He has let you in through baptism. He wants you to have all the gladness and blessing of working in His Kingdom, and making Him pleased, and making His poor children on earth happy and good. You are members of the Kingdom of God. Story—Frederick the Great examining school on the three great Kingdoms of Nature—Animal, Vegetable, and Mineral. "Now, what Kingdom does this belong to?" (holding up watch). "The Mineral Kingdom." "And this flower?" "The Vegetable Kingdom." "And now, what Kingdom do I belong to?" he asked. Expected answer, "The Animal Kingdom." But the children were puzzled. At last a little girl timidly held up her hand. "Well, my little maid?" "The Kingdom of God, your Majesty." And, amid solemn silence, the great King bowed his head. "Pray God that I may be worthy," said he.

How can you be worthy? How can you escape

disappointing our Lord? Get the strength for the Kingdom's work through prayer; through your Bible, through His great sacrament of Holy Communion for the strengthening and refreshing of our souls. You never can do His work faithfully without those helps. Try hard not to neglect them; not to get up late and run down to breakfast without prayer. Pray to the Lord, whom so many are disappointing: "Lord! I want not to disappoint Thee. I want to be a faithful member of the Kingdom of God."

QUESTIONS FOR LESSON XV

What was the chief subject of Our Lord's teaching?

Did He mean Heaven?

What did He mean? Show this.

Does it exist in perfection anywhere?

Prove this from Lord's Prayer.

What do you think of the Christian church on earth as compared with the vision He had in mind?

LESSON XVI

THE FOUNDING OF
THE KINGDOM

St. Luke VI. 12-26; St. Matthew V. 1-10.

§ 1. Trusting the Kingdom to Men

We have now learnt something about the Kingdom. Now how did He begin to found His Kingdom? By getting soldiers, and cannons, and swords to fight, as earthly kings do? No. His Kingdom not like that. You know now what He wanted done in the world; how would you begin if you wanted it done? He began by preaching about it, then by gathering together a few earnest, unselfish men and inspiring them with His own eagerness and enthusiasm for serving others.

Tell me the first of His new members (Luke vi. 14). Were they strangers to Him? (John i. 40, etc.). He had already made friends with them; they knew Him, and were in sympathy with Him, and were probably expecting this call some day to start at making the new Kingdom to bless the world. Very few. How was it like leaven, and corn, and grain of mustard seed?

But more and more disciples came as they heard Him, and saw the wonderful miracles. Tell me some of the miracles. At last time came for a solemn founding of the new Kingdom (Luke vi. 12-26). Did He mean to accomplish it all himself? No. He was leaving the world soon. Marvellous to say, He was going to entrust it to men. "I will trust them," He said, "they will rise to the trust, and I will be watching over them to the end of the world."

It was a splendid venture of God's generous faith in humanity which had so often disappointed Him. Don't you wish we were more worthy of His trust?

§ 2. The Choosing of the Leaders

Now it is the eve of the great Day and He had retired into the mountain, as was His custom—for prayer. He could not do without that. He knew what it meant to Him, this talking to the Father. And He knew what it would mean to us all through the ages. Therefore He keeps telling us to try it always. There on that mountain side, all night long, alone under the starry sky, He kept praying to His Father, and thinking of His glorious plan for the world. All night long alone, and then in the early morning, with the earnest light in His eyes, and great solemn purpose in His heart, He came down to a level place on the mountain-side. Crowds waiting, disciples waiting quietly, solemnly, as He came.

Then He told the whole band of disciples that He was about to choose twelve Apostles out of them to be the chief helpers in the new Kingdom. Imagine the breathless waiting to see whom He would choose. Imagine school captain of football team choosing players for a big match. Only this match was to be against the devil, and all the misery and sin of life. One by one He called the names, each wondering who would be called next. Peter! Andrew! John! James! etc. One by one they rose and came. How solemnly the crowd would watch. One of the greatest days in the history of the world.

That simple ceremony on the hill that morning was one of the great events of history, the beginning of a little society, the Christian Church, which should go out through all the ages proclaiming His Kingdom, the planting of a seedling in which He saw far off a great spreading tree with the fowls of the air lodging in its branches.

§ 3. *The Ideals of the Kingdom*

Then as the disciples waited in silent expectation "He opened His mouth and taught them" the ideals of the Kingdom (Matthew v. 1-12). The Kingdom of God was no new idea to the Jews. In ancient days it was their proudest boast that God was King in Israel. And their prophets always persistently pointed to a Golden Age, when there should be a Kingdom of God again. But naturally the people read their own low thoughts into it.

That coming day was to be a Day of Holiness, it is true, but prominent in their thoughts was "Der Tag"—The Day—somewhat in the German sense. A Day when

Messiah should lead Israel to victory, when the nations who oppressed them should bow beneath their feet, and Israel should rule gloriously. They already believed Jesus was the Messiah, and now He was going to speak to them of the Kingdom of God.

Then Jesus opened His mouth and taught them—not of triumph and revenge, and wealth and self-assertion. That was not His idea of a happy world.

> "Blessed are the poor in spirit, for theirs is the kingdom of heaven.
> Blessed are the mourners, for they shall be comforted.
> Blessed are the meek, for they shall inherit the earth.
> Blessed are they that hunger and thirst after righteousness, for they shall be filled.
> Blessed are the pure in heart, for they shall see God," etc.

§ 4. Depicting Christian Character

So Jesus proclaimed His Kingdom and its ideals. Remember similar scene in Old Testament. There God awful in lightnings and thunders. Here God in form of man, sitting as comrade beside them. Note the kindly form of the laws: all blessings.

Note, too, that they are, not a *command to do* something, but a *description of character*, which should be the character of the members of His new Kingdom. Note also that it is not each precept alone, but *all together*, that form that character. Therefore we must think of them connectedly. Now listen to the Laws of the Kingdom for the Apostles and disciples, and you and me, and all Christians.

1. POOR IN SPIRIT, i.e., feeling oneself poor, in want, needing help from God, deserving nothing. Remember any examples? (Luke xviii. 13; Romans vii. 24). Who will feel that most? Those who are trying hardest to be good. They must feel their spiritual poverty, and our Lord says that is a blessed thing. So with you. If you feel like that, it is much better than to feel proud and self-reliant about your Christian fight.

2. THEY THAT MOURN.—Does it mean mere mourning of any kind for more money, and more amusement, and more fame, etc.? No. Though every sorrow brought to Christ will be comforted in some way, yet here we must take it in connection with the "poor in spirit." It means that for the man who feels that need and demerit, it is a blessed thing to think about it and mourn for it. Every true boy or girl or man or woman who really sees the difference between what he should be and what he is, must surely mourn for it. That is blessed, says the Lord. What is His promise? That is the one sort of mourning of which we may be quite sure "he shall be comforted." But it is possible to hide it from ourselves, and not think or mourn about it. Too busy with lessons, and work, and play, etc. That is a pity. "He who lacks time to mourn lacks time to mend. Eternity mourns that."

3. THE MEEK.—This is the hardest part to teach boys. Boys don't like meekness. They sneer at a meek, chicken-hearted boy, always cowardly and cringing. Does our Lord mean that? Is it wrong to be angry with a cruel wrong-doer? Is it wrong to thrash a big bully for ill-treating a little chap? Certainly not. That is Christ's

will for you, if you can't stop him otherwise. Think of His own awful anger if one injured one of the "little ones" (St. Matthew xxiii. 1, etc.). But then, what about "meek"? It is the feeling that follows on the feelings in (1) and (2). He who knows himself, and how little he deserves, will not be always standing on his dignity, and making the most *of himself*, and flaring up at every fancied insult *to himself*. Meekness means absence of *self*-assertion. Stand up for weaker ones, and fight for them if necessary, but *not for yourself*. Our Lord dislikes your continually standing up for yourself. Did He ever do it? "Blessed are the meek" means "blessed are they who do not assert themselves and stand up for themselves."

4. HUNGER AND THIRST AFTER RIGHTEOUSNESS.— Same character still. He who feels his want of good, and mourns it, will be the first to hunger and thirst, etc., i.e., to eagerly, earnestly desire to be a noble, righteous boy. What is the promise? Grand promise? I think you all would wish to be good fellows, and please God. But a lazy *wish* won't do. Eager desire—*e.g.*, cycle race, football match—eager, passionate desire to win. As sure as you eagerly desire, says Christ, so surely shall you have it. Pray, "God make me hunger and thirst more, that I may be filled."

5. MERCIFUL.—Same character still. He who has (1), (2), (3), (4), must surely be merciful, forgiving, helping the weak, the needy, the unworthy. He who knows his own faults will be gentle with those of others. The world is full of people who will need your forgiveness and kindliness as you go through. The world is full of evil to

helpless classes. Child-life in cities, slum people living whole families in one room, poor old people beyond their work, etc.

6. PURE IN HEART.—Means more than common meaning of purity of life. Means "the will set straight towards God." But speak, too, in senior classes, of common meaning. Impurity, above all sins, shuts out vision of God. See this thought in *Idylls of the King*, where the quest of the Holy Grail was not for Arthur or Lancelot, or even Percivale; only for young Galahad of the white, pure soul.

7. PEACEMAKERS.—Boys and girls often the opposite. Instead of telling your friend the nasty thing someone has said of her, wait till you hear something nice said, and tell her that instead. What is the promise? Will you try to earn it this week? He who is really Christ's servant must always do it. It has a bigger meaning, too, which you will understand better when you grow older. "Not only curers of quarrels," says Mr. Ruskin, "but *peace-creators*—givers of calm, which they must first attain before they can give it." Some of us older people know some of Christ's servants whose very presence seems to make us restful and peaceful in our worries. Sometimes one's mother or dear old friend—a woman oftener than a man.

8. PERSECUTED FOR RIGHTEOUSNESS' SAKE.—Does not seem very blessed, does it? Yet it is wonderful the peace of conscience, the solemn, secret happiness, that Christ gives to the boy or girl willing to suffer for right. It is hard to be jeered at for saying one's prayers or for

rebuking filthy talk, etc. Poor coward would not face his comrades' sneers for these. But Christ's brave young soldiers of the Kingdom will do it fearlessly; and Christ is looking, and saying, "Blessed is he who suffers for the Right."

§ 5. St. Paul's Picture of a Christian

That is the character Jesus aims to form in us, the members of the Kingdom. Do you remember St. Paul's version of it twenty years after, His picture of a member of the Kingdom of God on earth (1 Corinthians xiii. 4)?

> "He suffereth long and is kind,
> He envieth not,
> He vaunteth not himself, is not puffed up, is not easily provoked, doth not behave himself uncourteously, beareth all things, believeth all things, hopeth all things."

That is Christ's vision of a happy world, His Kingdom of God on earth that He bids us pray for; "Thy Kingdom come on earth as it is in Heaven." Surely earth itself would be almost Heaven enough if His Kingdom should come.

QUESTIONS FOR LESSON XVI

Describe how Jesus began to found His Kingdom of God.

How many of the Apostles' names can you remember?

How many of the "Blesseds" which Jesus pronounced?

Boys don't like the idea of "meek." What does it really mean? and what does it not mean?

Can you repeat St. Paul's description of a Christian man?

THE PRAYER OF THE KINGDOM

St. Matthew VI. 9-16; VII. 7-12.

§ 1. About Prayer

Now when Jesus had gathered a little group into His new Kingdom of God and told them how God was always caring for them, then He told them not to be afraid to talk to God, to pray. I want you to-day to think about Prayer.

Suppose I had the privilege of consulting in every difficulty and trial the very wisest and best and richest and most powerful man in the world. Suppose he lived in my town and that he liked me and that he told me one day that he would give his whole mind to any matter I laid before him and consult for me to the best of his ability and with the keenest interest in my welfare and then would do for me the very best thing that could be done.

Don't you think I should often go to see him? And

even if he sometimes thought my wishes unwise would it not be a great thing to go and consult him, at any rate? I think I should be very often on his doorstep. Should not you?

Now lift that thought higher. Lift it up unto the Lord. Think if that Friend were greater than man, that He had all wisdom and all power and all control of everything in the world and, with all that, had such deep love and pity for me that even my sins and unworthiness could not make Him forget me.

Now stop imagining. This is all real. This is what the Lord Jesus tells us about the Father in Heaven. God is love He says. His fatherhood is tenderer than any human fatherhood. Go to Him. Speak to Him. Tell him everything and trust Him to do the best for you.

§ 2. How To Pray

Now read St. Matthew vii. 7-12. The Lord is here insisting on the need of earnestness in prayer. What are the three directions? (1) Ask; (2) Seek; (3) Knock— *i.e.*, (1) Desire: ask only what you want or care about; (2) Seek it: search for it eagerly, like a gold-digger for the gold; (3) Knock: keep on persistently, importunately. See story of man knocking and keeping on knocking (St. Luke xi. 5, etc.). Often our prayer so careless—our knock like a boy's "runaway knock"; don't wait for an answer. If we prayed as Christ tells us, we should get far more answers. How does He illustrate God's love? (*v.* 11). Like a parent, only "how much more" shall your Heavenly Father?

Does this mean that we shall always get whatever we like to ask? Would that be good for us? Would you think a parent good who did that?—*e.g.*, a little child cries for bread-knife at breakfast. Why does he think he should get it? Because he is silly and ignorant, and does not know what is good for him. What does wise parent do? So in *v.* 9 the Lord qualifies promise. "If a child sees a loaf-shaped stone or a coiled-up serpent, and wants it, thinking it to be a loaf or a fish, would father give it?" "No," said the people. Well, He says, God in the same way will keep from you foolish or bad things that you in your foolishness think good. So, in asking for earthly things, first, never act selfishly—*e.g.*, two boys competing for a school prize. Lord, give it to me! That is selfish, and unlike Christ. God does not listen to such. Second, always say: "Lord, only give me what I ask, if it be good for me, and according to Thy will."

But there is one sort of prayer with no limit? Yes; when we ask to be made good, and true, and noble, and lovable. Need not say, "If it be good for me," nor, "If it be Thy will." Why? Yes; we can have as much as we like of God, of goodness, of unselfishness. What a pity, then, not to have more. Fancy going into a bank, and being told you may have as much as you like, and coming away with a few pennies. What grand fellows you boys could be, what high, lovable characters you girls could have, if only you cared more. Just ask, and keep on asking, and seeking, and knocking.

> "It is only God can be had for the asking;
> It is only heaven that is given away."

§ 3. The Prayer That Jesus Taught

Then one day He taught His disciples a little prayer that they might always use (St. Matthew vii. 7-12). What do we call this? The Lord's Prayer. It was given as a *form* of prayer and also as an *example* of all prayer. *"After this manner* therefore pray ye."

Now we use that prayer regularly. Do we understand it? First *Our Father*. That is to encourage us to remember how much He cares, to make us feel: "I am His child though a very unworthy child. I am asking of *Our Father*, therefore I may be confident, but *who art in Heaven*, therefore I must be reverent and solemn."

Now, how many petitions? First, three, then four. Three about God and His will. Four about——? Ourselves. Which first, God or ourselves? What does this teach? God first, man second. God's glory, and His blessed plans for the world first, my wants and desires last. After this manner always pray. Our first feeling in prayer is, "O God, I want something very badly for myself; please give it to me!" God says, "No, my child, that is not the way to pray. First calm yourself: think of my will and my Kingdom, and all my plans for the blessing of the world. Don't be selfish. Say first, 'Our Father, help all of us together. Never mind me just yet. I want that Thy name may be hallowed, that we may walk before Thee as the great, all-pure, all-holy God. I want Thy Kingdom to come on earth, and Thy will to be done on earth, that life may be the lovely, blessed thing which Thou desirest. Never mind me, Lord, just yet; these are the first things I want.'" Is it easy to pray like that? No, but it will become so, and it will be the greatest blessing to our lives.

Does God let me pray for myself at all? Yes. What are the last four petitions for? Yes, these are our sore wants, and God wishes us to ask about them. But even there He guards against my being selfish. How? Can you see? Say petitions again. Is it "Give *me my* daily bread? Forgive *me my* trespasses," etc.? No, not *me* and *mine*, but always *us* and *our*. I think God must hate selfishness more than anything on earth. He is always watching to stop it even in prayer. Like a father hearing one little chap in his family always asking, "Father, *I* want holidays for *myself*," etc. Father refuses. By-and-by he learns to ask, "*Our* father give us all a holiday—not me alone: I would rather not get it if the others had to work—it would not be fair." Then the father, with glad heart grants the holiday—glad because his boy has learnt the spirit of unselfishness in his requests. Now tell me the two great lessons of the Lord's Prayer.

1. God and His blessed purposes first; I and my wants last.

2. Not *me* and *mine*, but always *us* and *our*.

Now take the petitions in order, and see if it be true that no one can truly pray them unless he is an earnest follower of Christ. *"Hallowed be Thy name."* Meaning? May we think of Thee and walk before Thee as the great, all-pure, all-holy God. Could you pray that truly without trying to be good? *"Thy Kingdom come, Thy will be done."* Where? On earth. How? As it is in heaven. Could you pray that truly without trying

131

to be good? Thy Kingdom come into all hearts—mine and everybody's—that we may be true servants of Thy Kingdom, and make life happy and holy for all. That Thy will may be done. By whom? Me and all others—as it is done in heaven. Think of one praying that, and then wilfully doing wrong. What hypocrisy! *"Give us our daily bread,"* i.e., give to me, and to all the poor creatures around me, even to the little robin on the window-sill; give to me and to them by means of me and of all who have power to help. What would you say of a man who prayed that, and then turned away from helping some poor neighbour in want? *"Forgive us,"* etc. What does this force you to do? No unforgiving person dares use it. It would mean, "Forgive me as I forgive," i.e., "Don't forgive me at all." *"Lead us not,"* etc. Imagine a boy using that prayer, and then tempting another to lie, or do something bad. So on through the whole prayer. Learn to use it thoughtfully, and it will lift up your whole life. Begin to-night. Either the praying will make you leave off sinning, or the sinning will make you leave off praying. You can't do both together, so wonderful is the power of the prayer taught by our Lord.

The writer had once an interesting experience. An old friend talking to him about prayer, said: "Do you know I have a curious little habit, all my life; keeping accounts with God. Here is my account book. Here on the blank left-hand page, I write any important petitions I have made, leaving the opposite page for the answers. Sometimes I write in the answer very soon, sometimes not for months, and there are some cases in which it seems no answer has come, but in this latter case I sometimes, looking back, suspect there was a good reason for it. Probably that prayer of mine was not a wise one."

QUESTIONS FOR LESSON XVII

Could you repeat my picture of the good and powerful man and show how it leads up to God?

Repeat verse about asking—seeking—knocking.

Do we always get whatever we like to ask? Explain.

How does the Lord's Prayer teach us to keep God first in prayer?

How does it teach us unselfishness?

Tell the story of the man who kept accounts with God.

A PARABLE OF THE KINGDOM

St. Mark IV. 1-20.

Jesus loved teaching by parables. Short, simple stories of which people had to guess the meaning. This one is intended to explain why the teaching of the Kingdom sometimes fails and whose fault it is.

Do you remember on that day of the strenuous life of Jesus (Lesson XIII) it began with His teaching the Parable of the Sower. We only mentioned it then, we have to learn it thoroughly now.

§ 1. Picture of the Sower

Close your eyes, and make this picture in your minds. A mass of people, in their bright Eastern dress, crowded at the quiet lakeside—a fishing-boat lying at anchor a few yards away—and One sitting in the fishing-boat speaking to the crowd. He and they together are watching with interest a scene upon the hillside behind. And yet it is a very ordinary scene. Bring it into your picture. A large field upon the hill-

134

slopes, with the rich, brown earth freshly turned up by the plough—a pathway running across it to the farmer's house—the grey rocks here and there peeping up through the earth—the bunches of thorn pulled up in the near corner, leaving many of their roots in the soil behind them; and above it all, the chattering and fluttering of wild birds over the head of a sower, as he scatters far and wide his golden corn seed.

Together they watch this scene, and then suddenly from the boat the Lord calls to them: "Hearken! listen!" Immediately they are all attention, wondering what He will say or do. "See that sower sowing his seed? See where the seed is falling, and what happens to it?" Again they turn to look at the sower in the field. Now what do they see? Where do they see the seed falling? How many different sorts of soil? Name them. Yes. 1st, on the pathway going up to the farmer's house, trampled hard through many years of tramping. 2nd, on *stony* ground? No; little stones in ground would not destroy growth—but *rocky, i.e.,* where the grey rock rising through the earth, shows how shallow the soil is there. 3rd, on thorny, where thorns had been grubbed up, leaving some of roots behind. 4th, on the good ground.

Now keep your eye still on the field. What became of seed on pathway? On rocky ground? On thorny? On good ground? Notice the first did not grow at all. The second grew for a while, and then died. The third kept on struggling in a half-withered, useless state. The fourth grew well, and bore good fruit.

§ 2. Meaning of the Parable

Now we may turn away from the field and the seed. The Lord wanted to teach by means of these of another field and another seed. This sort of teaching is called? Parable? What is a parable? Yes. Or it is a something in the outside natural world that is very like something in the inside spiritual world. Why are they so like? Because both worlds are of God, and He works much in the same way in both.

Some of Christ's hearers did not care about the spiritual world, and did not want to know anything of it. But some had earnest hearts, and were anxious to learn. How? (*v.* 10). "To you," He said, "who come with simple heart and honest desire to know, I will teach the secrets of the Kingdom of God." So He begins:

The Seed is? (*v.* 14), the Word—the Word of God. What sowing of it had just been going on? Yes; He thought of Himself like the sower in the field, scattering the good seed over that crowd of people—they were the field. Did the corn seed succeed equally well all over the field? Does the seed of the Word? What is wrong when it does not succeed? Is it the seed? No; the soil. Seed is all good. Both the wheat seed and the Word seed. God has given both a miraculous power—to live, to grow, to bear fruit. But the seed is tender, delicate, can be lost and spoiled by neglect, bad soil, etc.

Does anybody else act as sower? Clergy, teachers, friends, who speak to each other about holy things. Look round Sunday School now. See all the sowers in all the classes scattering the seed. Think of preacher in pulpit to-day, scattering seed through the church. Is it not solemn to think of the picture which our Lord gave of the hearts on whom it is sown? How many sorts? Like what sorts of ground?

§ 3. *Four Sorts of Soil*

Now take these four soils separately.

(a) The Pathway. When the Great Sower sows, by the Bible, or the preacher, or teacher, some falls on the pathway. Think of this class—this school—and say solemnly to yourself: "Some falls on the pathway." Meaning? Yes. That some—let us hope they will be very few—will let it fall unheeded on the hard, trampled surface—"in at one ear, out at the other."

Children in school, men and women in church, who will listen without a single sin brought to remembrance—without one resolve for a better life; without one wish breathed up to God for strength to do that duty brought before them in the message to-day. What an awful waste. Think of the poor heathen wanting it, and not getting it, and we so shamefully wasting it. But that is not the worst. The hard hearts will get harder by it, like the pathway on which the sower often walks. Next Sunday the surface will be a little harder on account of the neglected seed and sowing to-day. And who is watching to snatch it away? (*v.* 15). Did you ever feel him do it? Well, watch out next time. When some whisper of God comes in sermon or lesson, or in friend's advice, or in conscience rousing you to resist meanness, or lying, or ill-temper—if you refuse to receive it and let it grow,

137

it will not be there to grow at some future time. Then cometh the devil, like the fowls of the air, to snatch it away. Sometimes you don't feel him; sometimes you do. Sometimes the sharp end of the seed seems to stick in soil, to get a chance of growing, and you feel conscience pricking you to do something or resist something; but you refuse. You can almost feel the devil snatching away the good seed that was trying to get hold.

Why does any heart become like pathway? Whose fault? Is it God's? Whose? Yes. When Christ has warned us that heart is in danger of getting harder, the seed of being snatched by the angels of Satan ever watching us, then it is our own fault if we do not watch and pray and be earnest. Suggest to form the habit of silent prayer for preacher and people when sermon begins. If much done, would greatly improve both preaching and hearing.

(b) Next sort of soil? *Rocky*, not *stony*; remember the distinction. How did it grow? Fast, because of warm rock below, warmed by the sun. But then what happened? Now, what sort of people meant? Better or worse than stony? Better, received the word, thought it very lovely to be a Christian, touched to tears by thought of Christ's love. Very gushing, emotional sort of people, greatly moved at Confirmation or such times. But no root—no holding on. The important thing in religion is not warm *feeling*, but earnest *doing*—eager clinging to Christ. In the little acts at home, in the little temptations at school, always trying to be loyal. Some people can't feel very deep emotion about Christ's love; they feel almost cold-hearted. But they say—Never mind. In spite of coldness of heart—in spite of discouragement of trying to do right and failing—I will cry to the Blessed Lord, who is so good and so loving. I'd rather bear anything than be disloyal to Him! Blessed is he that endureth!

(c) Third sort—thorny ground. Seed sown where thorn roots remain, and both spring up together. These are still better than the last soil. They keep on caring to be good, but only in a half-hearted way. They are uneasy about religion, and give half the heart to God, and half to the cares and anxieties of the world. And so they have just enough religion to worry them; not enough to make them happy. But what are they to do? Must have cares about work and home and support and getting on in the world. Yes, but remember our Lord's advice: "Seek ye first the Kingdom of God and His righteousness, and all these things shall be added unto you." Settle first of all to give your heart to God, and then, as His child, work hard and hopefully at all worldly things. Put God first. Bring all else to Him that He may help and bless you, and then struggle and work will not sadden or harm you.

(d) And last of all we have the good ground. They who hear the word, and accept it, and bear fruit thirtyfold, sixtyfold, and a hundredfold. No time to talk further of this. Take away solemn thoughts about this sowing of God's seed. Pray to the Great Sower that we may not disappoint Him. Pray to Him especially for the teaching in this class and in this school, that in the harvest of life there may be fruit of our sowing.

"Lord of Harvest, grant that we
Wholesome grain and pure may be."

QUESTIONS FOR LESSON XVIII

Tell of the man whom Jesus probably saw and describe the four sorts of soil in that field.

Jesus taught a lesson from that about hearers.

What was the seed?

What sort of people were the pathway?

The stony ground?

The thorny ground?

The good ground?

Whose fault that all were not good soil?

Where have you ever seen a "sower sowing the Word"?

LESSON XIX

THE HIGH SCHOOL
OF THE KINGDOM

St. Matthew V. 21 to end.

§ 1. God's Lower School

Want to talk about God's school for the world, and the various classes, and the lessons to be learned. Did you ever hear teacher in school say, "Now you have learned that lesson. You remember it? Very well; then I am now going to give you a new lesson—a higher and more advanced lesson." Is anything like that in chapter to-day?

The Lord Jesus is the great teacher of men from the beginning; and in this chapter, at the founding of His Kingdom, He says: "I am going to give the world a new lesson, higher and more advanced than the last one." Where does He say this? Read ch. v. *vv.* 21, 22, *vv.* 27, 28, *vv.* 31, 32, *vv.* 33, 34, *vv.* 38, 39, *vv.* 43, 44. Which is the old lesson, and which the new? Where are the old lessons found? Old Testament. Who taught them? God Himself, by His appointed teachers. Were they

141

the highest lessons? No; only the elementary lessons for beginners. Now going to give new higher lessons.

Why not give higher lessons long ago? Do teachers in school begin by teaching Latin and Greek and mathematics to the little infant classes? Why not? Is it the incapacity of teacher or pupil? So they begin with the A, B, C, and then lessons a little harder; and so on, and on, and on, waiting patiently for many days, and months, and years, till the gradually growing mind of the child can take in the high teaching. Same in moral and religious training. Slave mission in Central Africa for slaves rescued from the Arabs—poor creatures gathered in from slavery and savagedom, with all their heathen habits strong upon them—with drunkenness, and impurity, and murder, and revenge, quite common, everyday incidents. Missionary cannot begin with higher teaching about loving enemies, and the duty of self-sacrifice, and the perfect consecration of the life to God. Why not? Would not be understood. Begins with lower lessons. "Thou shalt not kill, thou shalt not steal," etc.; and if he can impress on them the sinfulness of these things, he may consider himself for the time fairly successful. By-and-by he hopes to give the higher teaching. And meantime he will often praise them for actions which to us would seem very imperfect. Is he right? Yes, like teacher praising junior class for work which he would think very poor in senior class. By-and-by, when these poor heathens have grown into high-minded Christian men, will they think the old lower teaching wrong as they look back on it? No, they will see it as a lower stage which they have long since passed, but a stage that was a necessary part of their progress upward to the full Christian life.

Why am I talking of these gradual classes in God's school? To help you to understand the Old Testament. Some people are puzzled because the lessons are lower than in New Testament, and because praise is sometimes given for imperfect or faulty acts. A lady came to writer one day, troubled because the Old Testament did not forbid slavery, or putting away a wife, etc. "Why did not God give higher teaching?" she asked. Could you explain to her? Yes; we are in the more advanced classes of God's school now since our Lord came; but the child-races of men in the earlier classes were not capable of our higher lesson, and could only be taught as much as they were capable of receiving. They were often cruel to slaves, often turned away wife out of mere ill-temper. God said, through His inspired teachers: "You must not do that. You must be careful and considerate for the slave, and for the wife who is being put away." They were not yet ready for the higher commands—to set free all slaves; not to put away wives. But they were moving towards it. By-and-by still higher lessons came through the prophets. But they were all like monitors and lower teachers in the school, sent by the Great Master. At last the Great Master Himself came, and now that men had learned the lower lesson, He gave them the new and higher lesson, and the new and higher power to obey it. He founded a High School, with harder and more advanced lessons. Always remember that the coming of Christ made an enormous difference in the world— higher power, higher lessons, higher blessings.

§ 2. *The Higher School in the Kingdom of God*

Now let us take each of the six new lessons. (If not time, teacher should only take one or two.) For example, *vv.* 21, 22. What was the old lesson? Not kill; just as missionary with savage tribe to-day. At the least offence they knock a man's brains out. Missionary does not begin with "Love your enemies"—too high a lesson yet. Enough if at first he can make the man keep from killing—even if he scold, and rage, and get angry; yet, if he keep from killing or striking, it is a good lesson, and a great step gained. By-and-by teach higher lesson. Later he teaches higher still, and so gradually progress is made.

What commandment forbids killing? Is it enough for us children of the Kingdom to avoid killing? Have you ever broken the Sixth Commandment? How many people have you killed? If not, how have you broken it? Because you are in the higher classes you belong to the High School—to the Kingdom of God—and therefore more is expected of you. "I am not satisfied," says our Lord, "with your merely not killing people. I go down to the thoughts and intents of the heart. If you hate and revile, and have a murderous feeling, I put you down as breaking my law." So with all the commandments. (In this manner all the six cases given by our Lord can be taught. If there is time, there are many interesting smaller lessons in the chapter, but not room in this Lesson to write about them.)

§ 3. *How To Think of the Old Testament*

Thus you have to learn how to think of the Old Testament. The writer heard a man say lately: "I do not bother about the Old Testament. Only the New Testament matters, telling about Christ." Was he right? True, the New Testament is far more important—all about Jesus and His Kingdom and His Teaching. But the Old Testament is the foundation of the New. Long ago in Abraham's day, God chose out one people to preserve and hand down His religion for the world. Century after century He trained and disciplined and chastised and watched over them. He sent them holy prophets and teachers such as no other nation had. It was all a long preparation for Christ's coming and His Kingdom. So the Old Testament was the foundation of the New. The lessons are not as high as in the New, but very valuable lessons all the same.

The human race is like a great colossal man, born long ago and growing up gradually. He had to be educated gradually, then when Christ came He brought new power to be good. The Holy Spirit, Prayer, the new teaching of the Gospel, and with the higher power came higher demands. We are as it were promoted to High School now.

Because of all God's care, the Jews thought they were His special pets and that He did not care for other people. Was this true? No. God has no pets. It was for the sake of all the world in the future, as He said to Abraham: "In thee and in thy seed shall all the families of the world be blessed."

But especially is the Old Testament valuable because of its prophecies of the coming of Christ and of the coming of the Kingdom of God. Remember some of these in earlier lessons. (Go back and remind of these lessons in Lesson II.)

§ 4. Jesus Revising His Own Bible

Now notice a very daring thing. These precepts that Jesus was correcting and revising were in their Bible. Think of any man daring to correct and revise the Bible! Why could He do it? Because He was not a mere man, but God. Count how many times He says, *"I say unto you"* (*vv.* 22, 28, 32, 34, 39, 44). "Your Bible says such a thing, but I say higher things. Your Bible commands thou shalt not kill, etc., but I command higher things. I am not satisfied with that for you. You children of the Kingdom must aim higher."

Always remember that it was God in human form who thus revised His own Bible. No one else could. And remember that He expects higher things of you than of the ancient Jews. Because you have higher power given to you. The Holy Spirit of God is very near to you since Jesus came.

> "And His that gentle voice we hear,
> Soft as the breath of even,
> That checks each fault and calms each fear
> And speaks of Heaven."

(Here explain briefly about the Holy Spirit which means God speaking intimately in heart and conscience.)

QUESTIONS FOR LESSON XIX

Which gives the higher teaching, the Old Testament or the New?

What do we mean by "lower and higher classes in God's great age-long school"?

If one objected that slavery was not forbidden in the Old Testament what could you reply?

Where do we find Our Lord revising and deepening the meaning in Old Testament? Give as example, "Thou shalt not kill."

What is the chief value of studying the Old Testament?

LESSON XX

SOME PRECEPTS OF THE KINGDOM

St. Matthew VI. 25 to end, and VII. to v. 6.

§ 1. Fretting for To-morrow

Read *vv.* 25-34, noticing the command three times (*vv.* 25, 31, 34), and each time followed by a reason. First, it is needless; second, it is heathenish; third, it is useless and mischievous. This is not a fault of children, and it will need some trouble to interest them in it. Meaning of "take no thought"? Don't fret; don't be anxious. See Revised Version. When our Bible was translated, that was meaning of "taking thought."

A book of that time tells of an old city alderman who died of "taking thought," *i.e.*, fretting; and one of the wives of Henry VIII. is said (and I don't wonder) to have been always "taking thought." Does the Lord mean that nobody need be anxious about the future—even careless, wicked people who neglect their duty? He is speaking to His own disciples, who are loving God and trying to do their duty, but are anxious about result; and it is only to such it applies. See *v.* 33: "Seek ye," etc.—*i.e.*, when you are serving God and trying to live your life for Him, you may trust Him to take care of you, and go about as light-hearted as the birds of the air.

Do we not need, then, to plan and work earnestly to prepare for the future? Should we sit still, and leave it to God?—*e.g.*, a boy preparing hard for future business; a father planning and working about children's future. Ought they let it alone, and trust God for it? No, God would be displeased if they did. God has given them brains, and strength, and power to plan, and if they won't use them, they must suffer. God only means, "*When you have done your best* with the powers I gave you, *then* don't fret—trust Me." See illustration—birds of the air live in perfect light-heartedness. But have they not worked and planned? Have you watched nest-building in spring, and all the planning and contriving for the coming young ones? The little birds of the air do everything possible for the future, but with light-hearted happiness, "reposing unconsciously on the purpose of God." Do you know the little sparrow's song?

> "I'm only a little sparrow,
>   A bird of low degree:
>   My life is of little value,
>   But the dear Lord cares for me.
>
> "I have no barn or storehouse,
>   I neither sow nor reap;
>   God gives me a sparrow's portion,
>   And never a seed to keep.

"I know there are many sparrows:
　All over the world they are found;
But our heavenly Father knoweth
　When one of us falls to the ground.

"Though small, we are never forgotten;
　Though weak, we are never afraid;
For the Heavenly Father careth
　For the life of the creatures He made.

"I fly through the thickest forest;
　I alight on many a spray;
I have no chart nor compass,
　Yet I never lose my way.

"I just fold my wings at nightfall,
　Wherever I happen to be;
For I know that the Father careth:
　Dost thou know His care for thee?"

This trouble of fretting for the future is not yours yet. You are like the birds. But it is a sore trouble to older people, and maybe to you by-and-by. So look at the Lord's three reasons. Find me the first. (*v.* 25); *i.e., It is needless.* You fret about the clothes and food to support life. But He says, "Is not the life itself more important?" And you have to trust God for that. You have to trust Him to settle whether you shall live or die. You may as well trust Him for the lesser things, when you have done your best to provide them. The birds and the lilies, which cannot even do all that we can—cannot reap or sow, or store in barns—yet God takes care of them. Could not you trust Him to care for you?

Second reason (*vv.* 31-33), *It is heathenish.* The heathens have to be anxious, as they don't know of

God's care; but you have been taught to think of Him as our Father. Our earthly father cares. Is not God at least as good as he, and as safe to trust?

Third reason, *It is useless and mischievous.* If you fret about to-morrow, to-morrow will still have its own cares when it comes. You don't lighten them by fretting about them to-day. God promises, "As thy day shall thy strength be." Each day gets strength for itself. But if you put forty days' care onto one day, you are not promised strength for that. So people spoil their health, and their tempers, and their work by living in a state of fret, which is a result of not trusting God. Good plan to divide life into days, and "live one day at a time." Each morning pray, "Lord, I want to live a beautiful life *to-day*—to be unselfish, and kind, and pure, and true. I want strength to bear all troubles of *to-day*, and to fight all temptations of *to-day*. I will not trouble about to-morrow till it comes."

§ 2. The Beam and the Mote

Now we come to the Parable of the Beam and the Mote.

Read ch. vii. 1-6. What is condemned here? Does it mean you must not form opinion as to whether a person is good or bad, whether a boy is a sneak or a liar, or whether he is honourable and true? Can't mean that. See *vv.* 17-20, where He tells you to judge by their fruits. What, then, is condemned? The criticising fault-finding temper—seeing motes, looking only for faults and defects, like the carrion-fly on the meat, looking only for the diseased parts. It is God's will that we should distinguish between good and evil. It is God's will that we should condemn evil. What a miserable milk-and-water set we should be if we never rose in fierce, angry condemnation of selfishness, lying, trickery, meanness. Remember how angry He himself was at all such times. When we read the passage, we see at once that what He condemns is the fault-finders, who are quick and sharp to see failings, but quite blind to beauties and goodness.

What their punishment? (*v.* 2). Get same treatment from man, and worse still from God. He who is not tender and sorrowful about his comrade's faults cannot belong to Christ's Kingdom, nor receive God's forgiveness. Is this sort of person quick at seeing his own faults? (*v.* 3). Meaning of seeing mote, and not seeing beam? He is quick to see others' faults, and slow to see his own. Christ wants the very opposite. How does a boy or girl manage to be so blind to own faults? Partly does not like to look for them; partly because we have two different names for a doubtful act—one name when we do it ourselves; the other when some one else does it.

> What I call Rashness in another,
>> I call Courage when the act is mine.
> What I call Stinginess in another,
>> I call Prudence when the act is mine.
> What I call Uncharitableness in another,
>> I call Keen Judgment when the act is mine.
> What I call Revengefulness in another,
>> I call High Spirit when the act is mine.

And so on. Thus we manage to make little of own faults, and much of others'. Remember this danger, and watch against it.

Am I not, then, to speak to my comrade, that he may get rid of the fault I see in him? Yes; but what is the first thing to fit me for helping him? (*v.* 5). Be very keen and sharp-sighted in judging myself, but very gentle in making allowance for another. The member of Christ's Kingdom must be humble, merciful, sympathetic in judging—looking for good rather than evil, putting the kindest construction possible upon others' acts.

Are you to feel bound, then, to believe everything good of every rascal under the sun? No; but you are to judge like Christ, *i.e.*, to judge fairly, to look for the good in them as well as the evil—nay to look more for the good than the evil, even as He does. That is the great blessedness of dealing with Christ—He is so quick at finding the good: like magnet, so quick in finding the steel in midst of rubbish. Never think of Him as if He were only watching to find and pounce on evil in you. He is always seeking for the least trace of good in you—seeking more earnestly than the poor mother, who tries to find good in her wicked boy. That is, I think, why the Lord Jesus condemns the fault-finder so sharply—he is so opposite to God.

An old legend about His childhood illustrates this. Playing with the Nazareth boys in the evening, they found a little dog dead on the roadside. "What an ugly little beast!" cried they. "How dirty and bloody! What a nasty smell from him!" But when little "Jesus the carpenter's son," came up, He cried out at once, "What lovely white teeth he has; they are just like ivory!" In the midst of all the ugliness his eye caught the one thing beautiful. Whether the story be true we don't know; but it just describes our Lord, always looking for the good.

Therefore, try to be like Him, looking for the good. There is some good in every boy and girl, and man and woman, in the world, even in the one you most dislike. There is a great deal of good in some of them, if we would get more sharp-eyed to see it, and give them credit for it, instead of being sharp to see the evil, and give them blame for it. Think now of the persons that you think worst of, and see if next week you can't find some good in them or some excuse for them. That will please our Lord.

QUESTIONS FOR LESSON XX

What is the meaning of *Take no thought* for the morrow?

Why then does not our Authorised Version say straight out, "Don't fret"?

What three reasons does our Lord give for not fretting about the future?

Repeat text about the Beam and the Mote. What does it mean?

Am I then not to see plain open faults in another?

What is the first step towards casting out that mote in another's eye?

LESSON XXI

COMING DOWN FROM THE MOUNTAIN

St. Luke VII. 1-17.

§ 1. *The Roman Captain*

We have been thinking of Jesus on that wonderful day on the mountain during the last six lessons—The Founding of the Kingdom; The Sermon on the Mount; The Teachings about the Kingdom. Now He is coming down from the mountain, coming down the hill, to Peter's house after the Sermon on the Mount. "After He had ended all His sayings in the ears of the people He entered into Capernaum," and the twelve were with Him fresh from their ordination, with a new, deeper solemnity in their hearts, thinking, listening, observing.

They see a poor leper come to Him on the road, "Lord, if Thou wilt, Thou canst make me clean," and Jesus said, "I will, be thou clean." So He had made another man happy. That's what He was always doing.

155

An hour later they are in the town. The narrow, crooked street packed with an eager, admiring multitude following. On His way to Peter's house, He is stopped by a deputation of the Capernaum elders with a most unusual request that He would do a kind deed for a heathen soldier. The Roman captain in the barracks on the hill is greatly distressed about a young slave lad in his household, in terrible pain, grievously tormented and at the point of death.

Not often would a Jew ask favours for a heathen. But this is a very unusual heathen, a man with a big heart, fond of his slave boy, a man with a big soul, feeling the emptiness of his pagan creed and seeing in the Jewish worship of the One Holy God some satisfaction for his soul's deep needs. Do you remember the White Synagogue on the hill where Jesus preached on His first Sabbath? This generous heathen had built it for the Capernaum people. Such are the men of honest and good heart who, we believe, must always find Jesus, if not in this world, in the world to come. Such men are drawn to Christ like the steel to the magnet.

§ 2. Like the Old Gods of Rome

Of course this officer knew about Jesus. His fellow officer was "the nobleman whose son was sick in Capernaum." For months past he could hardly get through the streets with the crowds, nor miss the rumours everywhere about the young Prophet. But he felt himself an outsider, a sinner "of the Gentiles," therefore his Jewish friends interceded for him. "He is worthy that Thou shouldest do this for him, for he loveth our nation and has built us our synagogue."

And Jesus went with them, but the centurion, when he saw Him coming, felt that he had been too bold; surely Jesus must have strangely impressed this proud Roman officer, suggesting the legend of his old heathen gods coming down from heaven. He actually seems to have seen what the Apostles themselves hardly recognised yet—that this Jesus of Nazareth was more than mortal man. "Lord, I am not worthy that Thou shouldest come under my roof nor thought I myself worthy to come unto Thee. Only speak the word and my servant shall be healed."

Surely Jesus loved the humility of the man. "Lord, I am not worthy, but I need Thee and I trust Thee." That is always a safe passport to the heart of Jesus. Some people are afraid to come to Holy Communion. "I am too low and sinful, Jesus is too great and holy." Are they right? No.

> "All the fitness He requireth
> Is to feel your need of Him."

So He said to the centurion, "Go thy way, as thou hast believed so be it done unto thee. And his servant was healed from that very hour."

§ 3. The Funeral at Nain

That was a startling miracle, but it was as nothing to the happening of the day after. It must have been very exciting to follow Jesus in those days.

"The day after He went to a city called Nain and His disciples went with Him and a great multitude." Nain was a little mountain town in South Galilee, near the place of the witch of Endor, about twenty miles from Capernaum. The ruins of the old village are still to be seen nestling picturesquely on the slopes of Little Hermon and the remains of the old gateway where Jesus met the funeral and the ancient burial-caves about a mile away. Up the slopes to the town were coming Jesus and His followers. Everything looked bright, peaceful, happy. When suddenly the note of tragedy creeps in, they hear in the distance a sorrowful wailing and soon through the town gate emerges the head of a funeral procession. Such a very tragic funeral! On the wicker bier the body of a dead lad, bound in the white grave clothes, with head and shoulders bare, and at the head of the bier a stricken, tottering woman. "He was the only son of his mother, and she was a widow." Any one of us would be touched by the sight. Jesus especially would. He would know all about her and the previous funeral which she had attended. Whose? And the little orphan son whom that husband had left to her, perhaps her only boy—perhaps a little baby whom she had brought up carefully and proudly. Perhaps he was now able to support her as Jesus Himself had supported His widowed mother when Joseph had died. Surely His heart was going out to her. With respectful sympathy Jesus and His followers draw aside to let the widow pass with her dead son. She has no eyes for Him, no thought of Him standing on the roadside, His heart full of sympathy.

Think of all the mothers in the terrible war-time and the countless mothers through all the ages passing before Jesus with that dead son and like the mother of Canaan never knowing that He was beside them, thinking, caring. And of the deeper tragedy when the lad is spiritually dead, bound not in grave-clothes of linen but in bonds of imperious evil habits and the bearers, his careless companions, carrying him and his ruin, and the mother, sobbing out her broken heart, has no eyes for Jesus at the roadside. Remember that Jesus is always in the picture though she see Him not and that "He has compassion on her." There are plenty of such pictures everywhere. Somewhere at every hour is repeated the agony of King David in the chamber over the gate.

> "Somewhere at every hour
> The watchman on the tower
> Sees messengers that bear
> The tidings of despair
> 'Oh, Absalom, my son!'
> The boy goes forth from the door
> Who shall return no more;
> With him their joy departs,
> The light goes out in their hearts;
> In the chamber over the gate
> They sit disconsolate,
> And forever the cry will be:
> 'Would God I had died for thee,
> Oh, Absalom, my son!'"

§ 4. "Having Compassion on Her"

The central lesson of the story of Nain is this: keep Jesus always in the picture having compassion on her. Only that gospel can make such pictures bearable at all.

Now Jesus steps forward. He has "touched the bier and they that bear it stood still" and the words of power thrill through the dead heart and brain, thrilled through that spirit world where that soul had gone. (Notice that Jesus always speaks to the dead person direct: "Little girl!" "Young man!" "Lazarus!")

And "he that was dead sat up and He delivered him to his mother." "Wasn't it just like Him," as we familiarly say? We reverently mean, "Wasn't it just like God?" Does it not deepen our hope of the glad day that is coming when in the land of the Hereafter He will take each of these boys and deliver him to his mother.

§ 5. Why Not Raise All the Dead Boys?

Does the question come to some of you—Why doesn't this pitiful Lord raise all our boys? I don't think we ourselves would dare to call them back if we could. With all His compassion Jesus doesn't bring back the boys. Why He did it here we know not. I think it was unwillingly and for some great reason. Surely He would not do it otherwise. For if we are right in our belief that death means birth into a larger life, the evolution of a soul into a freer, nobler existence, would it not be like putting the chicken back into the egg, putting the child back into the womb, bringing the butterfly back to be a caterpillar again? Only three times He did it in the whole of His life. He only knew why, but we can reverently conjecture why He would not do it oftener.

So we keep the dead boy in our thoughts. We keep him in our prayers. We thank God for the larger life to which he has gone.

In that free growing life he will be well worth waiting for in the day when God in His own good time will "deliver him to his mother."

QUESTIONS FOR LESSON XXI

What claim had the centurion on the gratitude of the Jews?

What fine things do you notice in the character of this centurion?

Picture for me Jesus and His disciples meeting the Nain funeral.

Repeat the pathetic words describing the mother and son.

Why, do you think, Christ does not raise all our dead boys?

LESSON XXII

JOHN THE BAPTIST AGAIN

Luke VII. 17-29; Matthew XIV. 1-12.

§ 1. *The Baptist Comes Back into the Story*

Shortly after this great miracle of Nain (see St. Luke vii. 17, 18), Jesus was in a crowd preaching and healing sick and blind, when He saw approaching a couple of travel-stained men off a journey. When He called them, they said, We have come with a message from John the Baptist.

Are you surprised? Did you think John was dead? Or had you forgotten him since the great day when he had baptised Jesus and proclaimed Him to the world, "Behold the Lamb of God"?

No, John was not dead, but his death was drawing near. Herod and the Pharisees were seeing to that. But there had come a change. His influence was waning. Before Jesus' baptism he was the most famous man in Palestine. But just at the zenith of his popularity he had suddenly paused—pointing to One greater than himself. From that day his decline began. We read in a previous

162

lesson how his disciples were vexed and jealous for their brave silent master whom they loved, and we read his noble answer, "He must increase and I must decrease. This my joy therefore is fulfilled." (Teacher go back to Lesson VII and tell this part of the story.)

§ 2. Despondency in a Dungeon

Now we come back to the two travellers bringing John's questions. John was a prisoner in the Black Castle of Machærus. Why was he in prison? (Read here St. Mark vi. 17-20.) He had dared to rebuke the king for his wickedness about his brother's wife. It takes a fearless and righteous teacher to act like that, and kings are not very much accustomed to such treatment.

The queen was greatly vexed, and she made Herod seize the Baptist, and shut him up in the Black Castle at Machærus, on the dreary, desolate shores of the Dead Sea. If any place could break down the spirit of John—accustomed to the free, wild life of the desert— it was that prison. The ruined dungeons are existing still, with the holes in the masonry for the iron bars, to which probably John was chained. There he had lain for about a year when our story opens, with the chains, and bars, and the foul air of the dungeon around him, and outside nothing to be seen through the gratings but the black, bare rocks, and the dreary, desolate sea. No wonder fits of doubt and depression should come on him at times.

During this time he would, of course, be eagerly listening for news of Christ, wondering if Christ

THE HIGHLANDS OF GALILEE

were doing all that he had prophesied of Him. What? (Matthew iii. 12). I think John was puzzled by the gentleness of the Lord. Where is the axe at the root of the trees, and the strong winnowing-fan that should sweep the chaff into unquenchable fire? John was of the sterner, harder type—the fighters and wrestlers, like Elijah, like John Knox, like the many fighters for God who had not room for gentler thoughts. So he is puzzled about the gentle attitude of Jesus. He does not see that the time for the axe and the fan is only to come when all the gentle, loving means have failed.

Who brought him news about Jesus? (Luke vii. 18). Evidently his disciples were allowed to visit him. They told of wonderful miracles, such as the raising of the widow's son, but of other things too. They were jealous for their own dear master fretting out his heart in prison, while all men were running after the new Teacher (John iii. 26). So, I dare say, they would talk of the prejudices against Jesus, about His breaking the Sabbath rules, and eating and drinking with publicans and sinners. And altogether poor John, in his depression and misery, got puzzled and doubtful even about the Lord. "Could I be mistaken? Perhaps He is not the 'Coming One,' but only another messenger like myself. At any rate, I know He is from God, and He will tell me truth. I'll send two disciples."

§ 3. The Answer to John

So the two disciples started. It took about three days to get from Machærus to near Nain, where Jesus had just raised the widow's son. When John's disciples arrived, what was He doing? (Luke vii. 21). So they stood in the crowd, and watched the healing of diseases and plagues, the casting out devils, and restoring the blind.

After this it must have seemed to them silly to ask their question. But they do: "John the Baptist hath sent us. Art Thou the 'Coming One,' or look we for another?" What did Jesus reply? In saying this, He is really almost quoting the very words of two great prophecies which He and John had learned long ago (Isaiah xxxv. 5, 6; lxi. 1). He knew John would understand, and He wanted to comfort him. But he adds a little word of rebuke, too, at the end (*v.* 6). You see, it was very unpleasant, this publicly expressed doubt. His disciples did not yet believe very strongly on Him. He could not trust their faith. And now the strong, brave John, who had borne public witness to Him, begins to doubt. I think it would hurt and disappoint the Lord, and I think it would be likely to have a bad effect on the multitudes.

But was He angry with John? How do you know? (*vv.* 7, 8). I think it is beautiful to see the kindly carefulness to defend John's character to the crowd, who would be inclined to think less of him on account of his doubting message, sent in an hour of weakness and despondency.

And there is something else very beautiful. Did He praise John to his disciples' face? No; He even gave them a little word of rebuke to take back. But the moment their backs were turned He bursts out into the most enthusiastic praise of the poor prisoner. I hope somebody told John about this before he died. For a very little while after, you know, Herod sent and cut off his head; and I think it would be a great comfort if he knew what the Lord had said. Do you think he knows it now in Paradise? What is the lesson for us from Christ's dealing with John? The world praises a man to his face, and speaks sharply of him behind his back. The Lord does the very opposite, and He means you to do the very opposite. If your friend has a fault, don't be afraid to tell him to his face, because you love him and want him to be better. But never talk of his faults behind his back, nor let others talk of them to you; and always be more willing to give praise than blame.

What high position does He claim for John? (*v.* 11). Why? (*v.* 10). Because he was the herald of the King. True, He praises John for his own sake, just before for his firmness and courage. But all that would not make him "more than a prophet." So remember, in the sight of Heaven the highest honour comes through connection with Christ, being His servant, doing His work. Yet there is a curious thing about the little one in the Kingdom being greater. Wonderful what high value the Lord Jesus sets on this Kingdom of His, into which you and I have been brought! Such an enormous difference has been made in the world by the coming of the Kingdom and the King, that the greatest of the wise and holy men of the old world are inferior even to little ones in the Kingdom, inferior in position and privilege to you if you are Christ's true child. Not only new teaching, but new power, new life, has come into the world with Christ. It is easier for us to know about God, and easier to fight our sins, and to live high, noble, unselfish lives.

What is meaning of "This is Elijah"? (*v.* 14.) (See Malachi iv. 5.) God had prophesied that another Elijah should come. You remember about Elijah, stern, grim, and solitary, with his solemn message of repentance, and of God's wrath against sin. How he rebuked King Ahab for his evil deeds, as John rebuked Herod. They were of the very same type—stern, and fiery, and eager for right, and fearing nothing in the world, except to grieve God. So John was a second Elijah.

§ 4. Jesus Will Think the Best of Me Too

So the messengers returned to John. We know nothing further. We assume that he took fresh grip of his courage and hope and we hope that some one told him before he died what kind things Jesus said of him after the messengers were gone. "Among them that are born of woman, there is no one greater than John." Think of the generous Son of God saying that of his poor servant. Just when he was so ashamed of himself and his doubts, and whisper this to your own heart, If it be possible to say a generous word of me when I am ashamed of myself, I can trust Him to do it.

§ 5. How the Baptist Died

Not much time more remains to the poor captive for doubts or hopes. Death is very near, but he is to

167

have some curious experiences before the end. One day Herod surprised him with a visit, another day he sends for him to talk to him in the palace. He liked John and was influenced by him. I read that he heard him gladly and did many things because of him. St. Mark says that one of his reasons for keeping John in prison was to save him from the murderous plots, for Herodias hated him as only an insulted woman can hate. She did not forget. She could bide her time.

Her opportunity soon came. It is Herod's birthday. The stately hall in the palace of Machærus blazing with lights and around the table is gathered a brilliant assembly—his "lords and captains and chief estates of Galilee." As the night goes on the revelry grows fast and furious. Even the prisoner in his dungeon could hear it. And at the height of it all Herodias springs a new sensation by sending in her beautiful daughter, Salome, to entertain the guests, and to dance for them the sensual Eastern dances which no decent Jew would tolerate. The guests are applauding her to the echo. The half-drunken king is so pleased that he swears before them all that she may ask what she pleases, even to the half of his kingdom.

The excited girl goes to consult her mother and returns with a new, hard look in her eyes. And the drunken men are half sobered with horror as they hear that clear, young voice in the cruel demand, "I will that thou give me here in a charger the head of John the Baptist." Even Herod in his cups is sobered by the horror. Herodias has won out. She has trapped the king at last. His depraved notions of honour leave him no escape. "The king was exceeding sorry, nevertheless for his oath's sake he would not reject her. And he sent and beheaded John in the prison."

And thus at last came John's signal to retire from his noble ministry for Christ, in the moonlight call of the headsman in his dungeon. And the bleeding head was brought in before the revellers and the girl carried the ghastly trophy to her mother. And the disciples buried the headless body and "went and told Jesus." And the brave, lonely prophet passed into the Unseen to watch again for his Lord till two years later straight from the Cross came the triumphant Christ to preach His gospel to the dead (1 Peter iii. 18, 19), to unfurl His banner and set up His Cross in that mysterious Land of the Departed. There John met again "The Lamb of God who taketh away the sins of the world."

QUESTIONS FOR LESSON XXII

What was John's question to the Lord?

Do you think the worse of him for such doubt?

What excuse would you make for him?

What did Jesus reply?

Tell me of His generous praise of John.

Why was John in prison?

Make a word-picture for me about his death.

LESSON XXIII

THE CONSIDERATENESS OF CHRIST

St. Mark VI. 30 to end.

The whole Lesson is about Christ's considerateness. Do not underestimate the importance of teaching the lesson about holidays here. It is most injurious to young people to associate God's will only with work and school, and disagreeable things, and to fancy that He only "puts up with" play, and holidays, and laughter, and all that they enjoy. Apply the third section as a "parable of life," as indicated in the Lesson.

§ 1. Considerate for Tired People

Read *vv.* 30-34. Hold up hands, all who don't like holidays. You *do* like them? But does God? Does He not prefer work? You know your school work is God's will for you—sums, and geography, and Latin, and all hard lessons. God's will that you should do them well. But what about the amusements—the games, the fun in the play-ground—the Easter, and summer, and Christmas vacations? What about marbles, and baseball, and football, and cycling, and cricket, and tennis? (For girls, mention girl's games.) One great use of studying our Lord's life is the finding out His opinion about matters of ordinary life. Now, here we have Him and His disciples going on holiday.

The Lord had sent His Apostles on a difficult preaching mission through the country. They had just returned from their mission; dead tired after tramping from village to village in the hot sun, preaching and arguing with unwilling hearers. What did they tell Him? (*v.* 30). And even while they told Him, had they rest? (*v.* 31). Many coming and going; crowding, clamouring, bustling; "no leisure so much as to eat." And the kind, thoughtful, considerate Master knew it had been a hard pull for them, that there had been overstrain of mind and body, and that the best thing for them was perfect change and rest. And don't you think He needed it himself even more? He had far more work and strain than they, and the news that had just come did not make it easier. What news? (*v.* 29). (See also Matthew xiv. 12). His friend and forerunner John murdered by Herod. He knew it was good for them all to get away from the work and the people—away amid the fields, and woods, and mountains—to walk and talk together; to rest body and mind, and to commune with God. What did He direct? Come apart with me into a country place and rest awhile (*v.* 31). Were they not kind and thoughtful words? What do they teach us about our holidays, and rest, and recreations? That they are part of religion, as well as work is; they are God's will—God's pleasure for us.

Is it right to teach young people that only lessons, and work, and sickness, and disagreeable things are God's will, and not to tell them that the games, and amusements, and merry romping everywhere are God's will, too, so long as wrong-doing is kept out? Would your parents like to see you never playing, or laughing, or enjoying yourselves? Would God like it? Parents want you to enjoy life. Does God? Yes; far more than parents do. Not lazy, constant idling. He hates that. He delights in hearty work. But He delights, too, in hearty play after work. Therefore, always remember in the midst of games and holidays that God rejoices in His children's enjoyments. He intended the lambs to skip and jump in the fields. He intended you to laugh, and play, and be full of happiness. Only one thing He forbids in your play, because it would spoil your happiness and your lives. What? Sin. Therefore always remember that holiday time as well as work time is the will of a kindly God for you.

§ 2. Considerate for Hungry People

(Read *vv.* 34-44.) We saw His considerateness for tired people. Now see it for hungry people. Did He get the holidays that He wanted for Self and disciples? Did He get away from crowd to rest? Why? (*v.* 33). I wonder if you would like, just at holiday times when very tired, to find holidays stopped. So here. Crowds saw them going, and noted direction, and came swarming after them—no rest; no quiet. Did He get vexed? (*v.* 34). His whole thought always for others. Far away in the country, many miles from towns and shops. What did disciples say? Jesus too considerate to do so.

Doubtless very tired and faint himself after that tiring day. So could understand their weariness, and the misery of walking many miles to find a shop. Tell me the conversation (*vv.* 37-39). Astonishment of disciples. What could He do with so little food!

Directions about seating them—in *ranks*—word means "garden beds." Evidently they were placed in regular rows and squares, and, with their bright-coloured dresses, looked like a number of huge flower-beds. Why so arranged? That all should be orderly, and none passed over. Like arrangements at big school treat. How many "flower-beds" would there be if all fifties? How many if all hundreds? Women and children sat in other rows separate. Therefore, easy to know number (*v.* 44).

Now, see the gaily dressed groups, like garden-plots, a huge crowd, and the five little barley-loaves in Jesus's hands. How the people would stare and wonder. What could He do? First He looked up to Heaven and blessed them. His thoughts were always of Heaven and thankfulness. *(Refer here to grace before and after meals.)* Then? Gave to disciples and they to poor hungry people—men, women, and children. How thankful the mothers would be to see the hungry children fed by Him. How glad He would be, for He so loved children. But how could five loaves feed five thousand? We know not. With God all things are possible. Does He ever do that miracle now? Would you be surprised if I had seen it done last year? How? Farmer put in a bushel of corn in ground, and left it, and God made it into fifty bushels! That miracle is going on every year. It was nothing difficult to our Lord. It was His ordinary work. He is always doing it. So the "water turned into wine" (John ii.). Nothing strange or difficult in it. It is God's every-day work, only just done then in a shorter time. In vineyards of Italy the vine roots suck up the moisture out of the ground, and God turns it into wine. To us all these things are miracles. To God they are easy, ordinary things.

In St. John's account we have a solemn beautiful spiritual addition to this story (John vi. 22, etc.), where Jesus teaches on the day after the Miracle, "I am the Bread of Life," for souls as well as bodies. "As I fed weak, hungering bodies yesterday, so I am always feeding weak, hungry souls." This He does through His presence and His strength given in answer to prayer and especially in the great sacrament of the Holy Communion through which He in mysterious ways conveys to men His own life, His own self. This is a tremendous, magnificent subject. This lesson leaves little time for it. But teacher should say what he can.

§ 3. Considerate for Frightened People

(Read *vv.* 45-52.) Midnight. He is alone on mountaintop. What doing? Yes; He is always longing to be at prayer in communion with the Father. Praying probably for the world, for the poor people whom He had fed, for disciples. Where were crowds? Where were disciples?

How situated? Did He know and see? Did they know that He was looking at and thinking of them? Like the poor troubled, frightened people in the world to-day. Is He looking at and thinking of *them?* Do they know? Some do. Most people doubt or forget that there is One always looking down, caring more than their nearest and dearest for the hard struggle of life. Just as on the mountain-top that night, so always. What did He do? Why? Bring out the thought of His care and consideration in going to help and cheer them, and apply it to the help He gives to frightened strugglers still. "Be of good cheer, it is I; be not afraid." Carry on the story, and apply it as a parable of life. When they received Him into the ship, the storm ceased, and there was a great calm. Show how that happens still when we receive Him into the ship.

QUESTIONS FOR LESSON XXIII

What is all this lesson about?

What three classes of people was He here considerate about?

What does it teach about work and holidays in God's sight?

God is every year doing that miracle of increasing the loaves. Explain.

LESSON XXIV

AT CAESAREA PHILIPPI

St. Mark VIII. 27 and IX. 1-8.

§ 1. A Critical Week

We are to depict two great scenes in the most critical week in the training of the Twelve. There are discouraging things happening in the Galilean ministry as it draws near its close. The multitudes are less in evidence. The bigoted ecclesiastics from Jerusalem have been in some degree disturbing the faith of those kindly Galilean peasants and the time is drawing near when Jesus must die and leave His Church to His poor disciples to carry on. More and more He seems thinking about the end and preparing them for it. The end is drawing near and must not catch them unprepared.

So He devotes himself specially to them. We find Him wandering away with them to all sorts of secluded places, keeping close with them. Now come these two glimpses at the beginning and end of this most critical week.

§ 2. *Peter's Great Confession*

Away in northern Galilee at the sources of the Jordan lies the gay little town of Cæsarea Philippi, the fashionable resort of the rich people going for holidays in summer. But I don't think Jesus and His disciples came for holidays. I think there was a sad sense of opposition and unpopularity in the disciples' hearts as they followed Him while He taught. All their popularity and success dying away. Even some of their fellow-disciples deserting (John vi. 66). And I think the Lord's thoughts, too, were serious and solemn, though He would not feel discouraged, like the disciples. He was come to the last year of His life on earth, and He must soon go away, and leave that weak little band to conquer the world, and establish the Kingdom of God.

And with such thoughts, as they sat, probably in view of the great rock, one thousand feet high, which overhung the town, He suddenly breaks the silence with a question. What? "Who do men say that I am?" I wonder if the disciples themselves were all very clear as to who He was. But, at any rate, they had listened to the talk of the people. What did the people think? Tell me anybody who thought He was John the Baptist? (ch. xiv. 2). From Malachi's prophecy (Malachi iv. 5, 6), the rabbis thought that Elijah would come back again, and rise out of the middle of the Lake of Galilee. Like Tennyson's beautiful thought about King Arthur in the *Idylls of the King*. Others thought He was one of the prophets. What was disappointing in all this? That no one seemed to recognise Him as the Messiah—the

177

Christ—after all His time, and all His care, and love, and wonderful miracles. Was it not disappointing?

But there is another and more important question. What? "Who do ye say that I am?" Why more important? Because the whole future of the world's salvation depended on His little Church, which He should leave behind, being clear about this. What answer did He get? Who gave it? Was He pleased? I think *v.* 17 shows a delight and comfort in this bold statement. "These, after all, in spite of their stupid misunderstandings, do know who I am. Who has revealed it to them?" (*v.* 17).

Don't you see how everything depends on this? The whole foundation of Christianity rests on this grand assertion, "Thou art the Christ, the Son of the Living God!" All the beautiful words and deeds of Christ would not do us much good, however we admired them, if He were only a good man. But when the poor, sinful, sorrowful world learns:—This is God who is showing this unselfishness, and kindness, and self-sacrifice for others; this is God's nature that is being shown to us; God has not forgotten us; He can't bear to let us perish; He loves us, and has given His very life for us;—don't you see what a splendid revelation that is for the poor world? Remember that this whole gospel hangs on that.

§ 3. *The Transfiguration*

This little glimpse on that mountain gorge marks the beginning of a never-to-be-forgotten week in the schooling of the Apostles. It opens with The Great

178

Confession, "Thou art the Christ, the Son of the Living God." It was to close with a greater scene. The solemn climax of the Transfiguration, and that glimpse through the Veil into the Unseen World where Jesus belonged.

For we are told of its closing day that "after six days He took Peter and James and John and went up into the mountain to pray and He was transfigured before them." They were alone in the darkness of a summer night, high amid the slopes of Mt. Hermon. The Master was apart from them rapt in prayer. When they had said their own little prayers they lay down to sleep in their cloaks. Sometime in the night they were awakened by a sense of brightness and glory and a consciousness of strange happenings. And their eyes opened on a scene never given to mortal men before. They seemed to be in a new world. I suppose they thought they had died and gone to Heaven.

The Master was still praying and as He prayed the fashion of His countenance was changed. The Divinity in Him shone out through the vesture of flesh and His raiment became glistening, "exceeding white as no fuller on earth can whiten them." And through the veil of that Spirit World which had sent Him here came spirit forms, the spirits of Moses and Elijah, the great leaders of Israel who had gone in there so long ago. "They appeared in glory and spake of His decease which He should accomplish at Jerusalem." That Spirit World was keeping close in touch with Him as it is really keeping in touch with us if we only knew it.

They gazed and gazed in dumb astonishment to

the end, till the vision was passing away, then the irrepressible Peter could contain himself no longer. "O Master, let us stay, it is good to be here, let us make three tabernacles for Thee, for Moses, and for Elias." And while He yet spake a bright cloud overshadowed them and a voice came out of the cloud, "This is my Beloved Son, hear ye Him." And they fell on their faces and knew no more till Jesus came and touched them and they looked up and saw the cold dawn upon the mountain and saw no man save Jesus only.

The Vision was past. The gates of the Unseen had closed again and they found they had not got to Heaven after all.

§ 4. What the Transfiguration Taught

Reverently meditate for a moment on that scene. In what way do you think it might affect our Lord? There He stood rapt in prayer, "steadfastly setting His face to go to Jerusalem" to die. He needed His soul kept calm and quiet in the unruffled peace of that other world. Was this the answer to His prayer, bringing the Exile back for the moment to the precincts of His home, to hear the approval of the Father, to be glorified with "the glory which He had before the world was"?

Then think what it would mean to the bewildered disciples, how it would exalt and solemnise their thoughts of the Master that He who moved daily with them in human comradeship was reverenced and adored in that world above. And how near it brought that world to them. How could this Kingdom of God

180

on earth fail if that Kingdom of God in Heaven was standing by and caring? Look at these two spirit visitants who had left this earth centuries before now full of the great enthusiasms of that other life? Moses did not talk of Pharaoh and the Red Sea—nor Elijah about Ahab or Naboth's vineyard. What did they talk of to Jesus? "Of His coming decease which He should accomplish at Jerusalem." Does it not suggest how they and their great comrades within the Veil were watching eagerly their Master's life on earth and the great crisis of man's redemption, the greatest event in the history of their race?

And does not this thought so fully confirmed by our Lord, of the deep sympathy and interest of that other Land, help us to believe that our dear ones in that Spirit Land to-day, living and conscious and remembering, are watching and thinking of our life on earth and loving and helping and praying for us who are still in the land of shadows. Some of the greatest of the old Fathers of the Church loved to picture this. The galleries of the Unseen Land crowded with spectators looking down on our struggles. Like the old boys coming back on the anniversaries of a great school watching the games and conflicts in which they themselves had played forty years ago. See this thought in the Epistle to the Hebrews (Hebrews xii. 1). Seeing that this Spirit Land is watching the contest, "Seeing that we are compassed about with such a crowd of witnesses, let us run with patience the race that is set before us."

§ 5. The Boy at the Bat

Here is a lovely story I have lately met with: An old county cricketer had lost his sight, he was stone blind and it was his grief that he could not see his own son play the great game. The son used to lead his father to the ground, but he got small satisfaction from it. He could hear the cheering if his boy played well but he could see nothing.

One day he suddenly died and, contrary to all expectations, his boy turned up at an important school match to be played the next Saturday. He played that day a magnificent game. He batted as he had never done before and won the match for his school. During the applause a comrade asked, "How was it you played so magnificently to-day?" "Because," said the boy with enthusiasm in his eyes, "it was the first time my father ever saw me bat!"

QUESTIONS FOR LESSON XXIV

What happened at the beginning and at the end of this Great Week?

Tell me Jesus' question and repeat Peter's great reply. Why did this matter so much?

What is meant by the Transfiguration?

Two men appeared who had died long ago. What did they speak about?

What does this teach?

Tell me the story of "The boy at the bat."

FAREWELL TO GALILEE

St. Matthew XVIII. 1-8 and 21-36;

St. Matthew XIX. 13-15;

St. Mark IX. 30-38.

Then read St. Mark X. 1
to show He was leaving for Judea.

§ 1. *The Epileptic Boy*

We are drawing to the close of this Galilean story. That wonderful week in last lesson opening with the Great Confession and closing with the Transfiguration marks a new crisis in the History of our Lord. He seems different, higher, greater, more apart. He is contemplating the end. "As the time drew near that He should be received up He steadfastly set His face to go to Jerusalem" (St. Luke ix. 31). He has to go to Jerusalem to teach His gospel in the centre of the nation. He has to go to Jerusalem to die. The end is in sight.

Immediately after the Transfiguration is a picture not in our lesson to-day, of a great crowd and nine troubled disciples and a father heart-broken over his epileptic boy.

"Bring the boy to me," said Jesus. "Now tell Me how long he has been thus?"

"He has been thus from a child, O Master. If Thou canst do anything, have compassion on us!"

" 'If Thou canst!' Can you not trust Me more than that?"

And straightway the father of the child cried out with tears: "Lord, I believe; help Thou mine unbelief!" Surely a cry of faith that touched Him to the heart, what many a poor, honest doubter has cried since. And immediately the evil spirit was cast out and Jesus tenderly lifted the poor grovelling boy and gave him back to his father.

§ 2. "Who Shall Be Greatest?"

But Jesus was avoiding crowds just now. He was keeping His disciples in retreat for solemn private teaching. No chance of remaining in retreat now that the people have discovered Him. So they start homeward to Capernaum. The days in Capernaum are fast drawing to a close. St. Mark tells (ix. 30) how He tried to avoid recognition on His way back by untrodden ways that He would not that any man should know and on the way He told again of His approaching death.

But they did not seem to understand, for on the way they talked of a very different subject. On the road the Lord overheard a dispute going on behind him. They thought He had not heard. They were utterly confused and ashamed, when, as they sat in the house, He quietly turned to ask them—what? Felt like school-boys caught in some wrong that they thought was not known. Already they had learned enough to be ashamed of the dispute. What was it about? Why this dispute now? Perhaps because, Peter, James, and John were chosen to be at Transfiguration. Perhaps the high praise given to Peter at Cæsarea Philippi. This account in St. Matthew begins: "Who, *then*, is greatest?" (see R.V.). The "then" makes one think that there has been previous talk of it. Perhaps they think, if we may not *dispute*, at any rate we may *inquire*. So they ask, "Who, then, is greatest?" But the whole discussion shows how totally they misunderstood the beautiful self-sacrifice which He was always trying to teach them—showed a selfish, earthly spirit. The Lord was sorry to see this bad spirit. Tried to teach them the law of greatness of the Kingdom of Heaven—what? (*v.* 4). Meaning? THE HIGHEST GREATNESS IN GOD'S SIGHT IS THAT OF HUMBLING AND FORGETTING SELF FOR THE SERVICE OF OTHERS. THE LOWEST POSITION IN GOD'S SIGHT IS HIS WHO IS ONLY STRIVING AND STRUGGLING FOR HIS OWN GAIN AND GREATNESS.

§ 3. *The Heart of a Little Child*

How did He begin teaching this lesson? Called to Him a little child, perhaps one of Peter's small boys, as this was probably Peter's house in Capernaum (Mark ix. 33). Did the child come? Yes. I think any child who knew Him would have run to Him. I can

185

imagine the boy, in his little striped tunic, with bare arms and legs, running to Him at once. Don't you think the children in that house would be fond of the Lord Jesus who often came in amongst them? Do you think children soon find out who is fond of them? Some people don't care for children. Some greatly love them—which sort our Lord?

Did He tell the little chap to stand away from Him while He taught this lesson? What then? Lifted him on His knee; put His arms around him (Mark ix. 36). I don't think He could help doing that whenever He got a little child near Him (see Mark x. 16). He was so fond of them, they could not help being fond of Him. You could not either, if you saw Him and knew Him, as you will one day in heaven. He was very popular with children. They ran to Him, clung to Him in His arms, shouted "Hosanna" to Him. What a kindly friend for children. Full of sympathy for their innocent pleasure and mirth.

Think of these apostles, each worrying and striving to be greater than the others. See them looking at this innocent little child taken from his play, and wondering in his little heart how he came to be taken such notice of. No thought in *his* mind about their wretched strivings and ambitions. Quietly nestling in the arms of Jesus; living in the present, not fretting about the future, he is just the example to teach them Christ's lesson: "Unless ye become like this child." How? Does it mean that child sinless? Or any child? (Tradition—This child was afterwards the great martyr, St. Ignatius, thrown to wild beasts in Rome. Perhaps true. Probably fond enough of our Lord to die for Him.) But surely not sinless. Even little children need a Saviour. But the Lord wanted to teach child-like spirit. Children, unless badly brought up, are innocent, contented, kindly—not self-conscious, not supercilious, or making class distinctions. Not fretting about the future. Peacefully, quietly trusting their parents, and living just "one day at a time." The hard world hardens and spoils us. The Lord says, "Keep the child-like heart in you. Be as little children in the Great Father's home. Not worrying or fretting for greatness, but loving and trusting the Father, and gladly doing His will." What is the secret of the child being so happy and child-like? *He is sure that he is loved.* Our first great lesson to learn in God's service is that. Be sure that you are loved, more than by parent or dearest friend. That is a more important lesson even than to learn that you are sinful. Nothing helps us like feeling that we are loved and cared for. Jesus says that to be religious is to be just like that in the Father's house; that it is especially pleasant in the sight of God to have the heart of a little child.

§ 4. Guardian Angels

But there are other lessons to teach from the text of Peter's little boy. As the child nestled in His arms He is looking into the future, to the innocent children grown to evil manhood or womanhood through enticement or evil example of others. Even we ourselves would feel vexed at that. It is something to think that God feels even as we do. "It were better," said the indignant Christ, "for a man to have a mill-stone tied round his neck and to be cast into the sea than that he should mislead one of my little ones. Take heed that ye despise them not, for in heaven their guardian angels do always behold the face of My Father which is in heaven."

Do you wonder what that means? I think it means that we have each guardian angels that have special charge of us. I sometimes wonder if they are not our own beloved ones who have gone, each of them caring for his own. I think that very likely, for as they are alive and remembering us they must surely care and probably they think and pray and help us more than we know.

§ 5. *"Suffer Little Children"*

I place here on one of these days of His farewell to Capernaum that other delightful little picture of the children brought to Him for blessing before He departed. The story stands in the gospels (St. Matthew xix. 13-15) without mark of time or place, except that it was about this period and that He was just going away from somewhere at the time. I think of the mothers of Capernaum sorry that He is going, whom their children are fond of, and wanting His farewell blessing for the little ones. They are lingering about the door where He is teaching His solemn lessons to the disciples and these self-important disciples are indignant that He should be disturbed by mere women and children.

This is one of the few times He is angry with them. "When Jesus saw it, He was much displeased and said, 'Suffer little children to come unto Me, for of such is the Kingdom of Heaven,' and He took them up in His

188

arms, put His hands upon them and blessed them, and He departed thence."

§ 6. *About Forgiveness*

We note a few more traces of teaching before He left. One day John asked Him "Were we right in forbidding a man who followeth not with us to teach in Thy name?" Jesus said, "Forbid him not, he that is not against us is on our side."

Another day Peter wanted to know about forgiveness. "How oft must I forgive? Till seven times?" "Nay," said Jesus, "but until seventy times seven." There must be no end to forgiving. For how can a man forgiven so greatly by God, forgiven ten thousand talents—take his brother by the throat who owes him a hundred pence?

He tells them a parable that should force any man to forgive. Tell it me very carefully—every point is important. Now for meaning. Who is the King? What is the reckoning? No. I think not the Day of Judgment, else how could the rest of parable happen? Sometimes God's Holy Spirit makes one feel one's sin deeply— reckons it up to him, like a kind creditor, who wants to save one from going too much in debt. This sinner asks God—what? No, not to let him off, but give him time. He thinks he can pay off his debt by being good in future. Can he? He is bound to be good in future, any way; and what of his past? What does God do? Forgave it all. Why? Because man could not pay. Moved with compassion. Fancy forgiving a huge debt like that— more than a million pounds. That means that every one who is neglecting God's service, who is accepting God's gifts, health and strength and brains and abilities and then using God's gift for evil or for selfishness, owes a tremendous debt to God.

Think of any man forgiven all that debt refusing to forgive another for some small fault.

Whenever you understand how great and full is God's forgiveness, you will be so touched by it that you can never be unforgiving to another. You would feel as mean as the man in the parable. Is there anything that could ever make Him withdraw that forgiveness? (*v.* 35). What then is the rule of forgiveness? Even as God for Christ's sake hath forgiven you. What does the Lord's Prayer bid us pray about forgiveness?

§ 7. Farewell to Galilee

So in careful teaching, in close intercourse passed those last days in Capernaum. Little of miracles or public teaching. Jesus and His twelve men together.

Before He departs let us glance at the position. Galilee was on the whole a disappointment, though we must not forget that He got eleven of His twelve Apostles there. At first they received Him gladly. They liked Him for Himself and also they hoped that He would restore the Kingdom to Israel and conquer all their oppressors. But that was not His purpose. So He disappointed them as they disappointed Him. To the end the Galilee people loved Him and championed Him even in Jerusalem. But they were not much in earnest. Not bad people, but like so many others, careless, indifferent.

Jesus is going on now to face what His destiny has still in store. "Now that the time was come that He should be received up He steadfastly set His face to go to Jerusalem, sadly He bids goodbye to His native province, which had failed Him. As He sorrowed later over Jerusalem, so He sorrows now over these pleasant places by the Lake, His home through many vicissitudes for more than a year. He is so sorry for what they have missed. If they had only known! If they had only known!

One can picture Him on the Jerusalem road turning back for a last look. "Woe for thee Chorazin, woe for thee Bethsaida, and thou Capernaum, who wast exalted to heaven shall be cast down to Hades. For if the mighty works done in thee had been done in Sodom it had remained to this day."

QUESTIONS FOR LESSON XXV

Why did they come back to Capernaum by lonely roads?

What did the disciples dispute about?

Jesus used a little child as a text for His sermon to them. How?

Tell me the parable about forgiveness. Explain it.

Where was the Lord going to and why, when He bade farewell to Galilee?

CPSIA information can be obtained
at www.ICGtesting.com
Printed in the USA
BVHW04s1511190518
516623BV00001B/71/P